W9-BOP-045

TWO GREAT WRITERS
OF COMEDY

The plays in this volume reflect the drive
and vitality of their creators, whose
careers swerved from adventure to
misadventure, from gaiety to misery. Lovers
of life and living, bursting with energy,
mirth and wit, Goldsmith and Sheridan,
while products of their times, both
rebelled against the confines of the age.
Implicit in their works is a defiant and
ironic shout at the sentimentality and
humorlessness of eighteenth-century
England. To this day, their works continue
to delight a too-sober world.

SHE STOOPS TO CONQUER

BY OLIVER GOLDSMITH

THE SCHOOL FOR SCANDAL

BY RICHARD BRINSLEY SHERIDAN

BANTAM BOOKS, INC.

BANTAM PATHFINDER EDITIONS
NEW YORK / TORONTO / LONDON

RLI: $\dfrac{\text{VLM } 8.0}{\text{IL } 9.12}$

SHE STOOPS TO CONQUER &
THE SCHOOL FOR SCANDAL
Bantam Pathfinder edition published November 1966

Bantam Books are published by Bantam Books, Inc., a subsidiary
of Grosset & Dunlap, Inc. Its trade-mark, consisting of the words
"Bantam Books" and the portrayal of a bantam, is registered in the
United States Patent Office and in other countries. Marca Registrada.
Bantam Books, Inc., 271 Madison Avenue, New York, N.Y. 10016.

PRINTED IN THE UNITED STATES OF AMERICA

Contents

Introduction

by
Brooks Atkinson

English playwriting during the eighteenth century generally lacked distinction. The public mood was changing. In Restoration times the theatres had been appendages of the court and were concerned with the amusement of fashionable people. But the rise of the middle class and the new prosperity of the merchants, many of whose daughters married into the aristocracy, brought new audiences into the theatre—people less interested in manners and style. Farquhar and Vanbrugh continued the Restoration tradition, but softened it to please a less sophisticated public. In 1728 John Gay wrote *The Beggar's Opera*—an ironic musical play that satirized Sir Robert Walpole, prime minister, and other officials of state and town. To this day *The Beggar's Opera* remains a notable marriage of dainty melody and mordant satire. Henry Fielding, author of *Tom Jones,* a lively man of letters and an alert citizen, also wrote a few farces, as did Samuel Foote, a celebrated mountebank whom Dr. Johnson regarded as an uproarious comic.

But playwriting as a whole relapsed into sentimental, mawkish drama to suit the taste of the great public. It was a drama of "cautious purity," in the phrase of Hazlitt. This was the period of the House of Hanover—at that time a heavy, humorless line of kings who were more Germanic than English and had undistinguished tastes in literature.

Not every one was satisfied with the pious sobriety of the theatre. In 1772, Oliver Goldsmith, an Irishman who was supporting himself in London by hackwork, attacked the prevailing style with a plea for the return of comedy. *Essay on the Theatre; or A Comparison Between Laughing and Sentimental Comedy,* he called his polemic. He had already tried to do something about it with a humorous, though un-even, comedy entitled *The Good Natur'd Man.* Since it was not solemn or genteel, it was regarded as "low."

But no one could resist his *She Stoops to Conquer; or, The Mistakes of a Night,* which was acted at Covent Garden in 1773. Its natural good temper and drollery, which are still captivating, reflect the Irish temperament of the well-loved author of *The Vicar of Wakefield* and *The Deserted Village. She Stoops to Conquer* owes nothing to the witty world of the Restoration dramatists. Its country humors are closer to Shakespeare.

Goldsmith was an improvident, impulsive, random sort of man whose misadventures were not unlike those found in his play. The plot of *She Stoops to Conquer* is in fact de-rived from one of his own experiences, for, like Marlow in the play, he once swaggered into a private home under the impression that he had entered an inn and commanded his host after the manner of a paying guest. Much of what we know about Goldsmith's personality comes from Boswell's *Life of Samuel Johnson, LL.D.* Since Boswell was obviously jealous of Goldsmith, we cannot take everything that he says at face value. Dr. Johnson had a high opinion of Goldsmith and more than once straightened out his muddled affairs. In fact, Johnson intervened with the manager of the Covent Garden Theatre to get *She Stoops to Conquer* on the stage after Goldsmith had bungled the transaction by recalling the manuscript and sending it to Garrick.

But Goldsmith was a lovable soul. When he died the next year, of a fever complicated by worry over his enormous debts, his friends in the Literary Club were deeply distressed. Sir Joshua Reynolds, the portrait painter, threw down his brush when he heard the dismal news, retreated into silence, and remained disconsolate for a long time. *She Stoops to Conquer* preserves the sunniness that attached Goldsmith's friends to him.

The English comedy of manners had one more day of brilliance before an eclipse of more than a century. In 1777 Richard Brinsley Sheridan put on *The School for Scandal.* Like Goldsmith, Sheridan was Irish. Sheridan was an attrac-tive, alert young man with a knack for shining in public, no matter what he was doing. Although he never appeared on the stage, his whole life was a dazzling performance.

When he was twenty-two he concluded a story-book courtship (which included two duels) by marrying the in-comparable Elizabeth Linley, a beautiful concert singer who had innumerable admirers, all of whom, except Sheridan, had the means to support her. Two years later, when, as usual, he was desperately in need of money, he wrote *The Rivals*—a comedy only a little less famous than his great one. The next year, when he was twenty-five, he purchased the Drury Lane Theatre, which was worth thirty or forty times his total financial resources. When he was twenty-six he gave it the most ingenious and successful comedy of his time—*The School for Scandal*, which has never long been off the stage in two centuries.

Its form is that of the Restoration comedy of the previous century, but in conformity with the moral tone of the Age of Johnson, and with Sheridan's own tastes in manners, the comedy is decent. Its standards of conduct reflect Sheridan's generous nature. In contrast with the brittleness of Restoration writing, the style has grace, flow and sensibility; and a certain undertone of amiability makes it winning as well as amusing. Sheridan was a fastidious workman. All his public performances, whether as writer or man of the world, had an easy, spontaneous style. But the aptness of the phrasing in *The School for Scandal* and the dexterity of the narrative represent the intensity of his craftsmanship. In addition to *The Rivals* and *The School for Scandal* he wrote one other sparkling work—*The Critic* in 1779. During the four years when he was working in the theatre he also wrote two or three potboilers.

But from 1779 to his death in 1816 he squandered most of his energy on a political career. As a member of Parliament he gave one memorable address, the Begum speech, which resulted in the impeachment of Warren Hastings. It was his last electrifying performance. Bad luck, recklessness about money, amorous entanglements, excessive drinking, and general irresponsibility left him a rather unsavory man in his middle age. During the twilight of Sheridan's career, Byron had this to say about him: "Whatever he tried he did better than anyone else. He wrote the best comedy, *The School for Scandal*, the best opera, *The Duenna*, the best farce, *The Critic*, and the best address, the Monologue on Garrick. And to crown it all, he delivered the very best oration ever conceived or heard in this country, the famous Begum speech."

But his twenties had been his triumphant period. His last years were as distressing as the last panels in Hogarth's *The Rake's Progress*. Sheridan left no successors in the writing of comedy. After *The School for Scandal*, the English comedy of manners took a long sleep until Oscar Wilde roused it with *Lady Windermere's Fan* in 1892.

She Stoops to Conquer

or, The Mistakes of a Night

by
Oliver Goldsmith

To SAMUEL JOHNSON, L.L.D.

DEAR SIR,

By inscribing this slight performance to you, I do not mean so much to compliment you as myself. It may do me some honor to inform the public that I have lived many years in intimacy with you. It may serve the interests of mankind also to inform them that the greatest wit may be found in a character without impairing the most unaffected piety.

I have, particularly, reason to thank you for your partiality to this performance. The undertaking a comedy, not merely sentimental, was very dangerous; and Mr. Colman, who saw this piece in its various stages, always thought it so. However, I ventured to trust it to the public; and though it was necessarily delayed till late in the season, I have every reason to be grateful.

> I am, Dear Sir,
> Your most sincere friend,
> And admirer,
> OLIVER GOLDSMITH.

PROLOGUE

By David Garrick, Esq.

Enter Mr. Woodward,[1] *Dressed in black, and holding a handkerchief to his eyes.*

Excuse me, sirs, I pray—I can't yet speak—
I'm crying now—and have been all the week!
'Tis not alone this mourning suit, good masters;
I've that within—for which there are no plasters!
Pray would you know the reason why I'm crying?
The Comic Muse, long sick, is now a-dying!
And if she goes, my tears will never stop;
For as a player, I can't squeeze out one drop.
I am undone, that's all—shall lose my bread—
I'd rather, but that's nothing—lose my head.
When the sweet maid is laid upon the bier,
Shuter[2] and I shall be chief mourners here.
To her a mawkish drab of spurious breed,
Who deals in sentimentals will succeed!
Poor Ned and I are dead to all intents,
We can as soon speak Greek as sentiments!
Both nervous grown, to keep our spirits up,
We now and then take down a hearty cup.
What shall we do?—If comedy forsake us!
They'll turn us out, and no one else will take us;
But why can't I be moral?—Let me try—
My heart thus pressing—fixed my face and eye—
With a sententious look, that nothing means,
(Faces are blocks, in sentimental scenes)
Thus I begin—*All is not gold that glitters,*
Pleasure seems sweet, but proves a glass of bitters.
When ignorance enters, folly is at hand;

3

Learning is better far than house and land.
Let not your virtue trip, who trips may stumble,
And virtue is not virtue, if she tumble.
    I give it up—morals won't do for me;
To make you laugh I must play tragedy.
One hope remains—hearing the maid was ill,
A *doctor* comes this night to show his skill.
To cheer her heart, and give your muscles motion,
He in *five draughts* prepared, presents a potion:
A kind of magic charm—for be assured,
If you will *swallow* it, the maid is cured:
But desperate the doctor, and her case is,
If you reject the dose, and make wry faces!
This truth he boasts, will boast it while he lives,
No *poisonous drugs* are mixed in what he gives;
Should he succeed, you'll give him his degree;
If not, within he will receive no fee!
The college, *you*, must his pretensions back,
Pronounce him *regular*, or dub him *quack*.

DRAMATIS PERSONÆ

SIR CHARLES MARLOW.
YOUNG MARLOW, his son.
HARDCASTLE.
HASTINGS.
TONY LUMPKIN.
DIGGORY.

MRS. HARDCASTLE.
MISS HARDCASTLE.
MISS NEVILLE.
MAID.
Landlord, Servants, &c., &c.

ACT I

SCENE I: *A Chamber in an old-fashioned House.*

Enter MRS. HARDCASTLE *and* MR. HARDCASTLE.

Mrs. Hardcastle. I vow, Mr. Hardcastle, you're very particular. Is there a creature in the whole country but ourselves that does not take a trip to town now and then to rub off the rust a little? There's the two Miss Hoggs and our neighbour, Mrs. Grigsby, go to take a month's polishing every winter.

Hardcastle. Ay, and bring back vanity and affectation to last them the whole year. I wonder why London cannot keep its own fools at home. In my time, the follies of the town crept slowly among us, but now they travel faster than a stage-coach. Its fopperies come down, not only as inside passengers, but in the very basket.

Mrs. Hardcastle. Ay, *your* times were fine times, indeed; you have been telling us of *them* for many a long year. Here we live in an old rumbling mansion that looks for all the world like an inn, but that we never see company. Our best visitors are old Mrs. Oddfish, the curate's wife, and little Cripplegate, the lame dancing-master. And all our entertainment your old stories of Prince Eugene and the Duke of Marlborough. I hate such old-fashioned trumpery.

Hardcastle. And I love it. I love every thing that's old: old friends, old times, old manners, old books, old wine; and, I believe, Dorothy, (*taking her hand*) you'll own I have been pretty fond of an old wife.

Mrs. Hardcastle. Lord, Mr. Hardcastle, you're for ever at your Dorothy's and your old wife's. You may be a Darby, but I'll be no Joan,[3] I promise you. I'm not so old as you'd make me, by more than one good year. Add twenty to twenty, and make money of that.

Hardcastle. Let me see; twenty added to twenty, makes just fifty and seven.

Mrs. Hardcastle. It's false, Mr. Hardcastle: I was but twenty when I was brought to bed of Tony, that I had by Mr. Lumpkin, my first husband; and he's not come to years of discretion yet.

Hardcastle. Nor ever will, I dare answer for him. Ay, you have taught him finely!

Mrs. Hardcastle. No matter, Tony Lumpkin has a good

(a) The *unturtered aristocracy*

(b) fortune. <u>My son is not to live by his learning</u>. I don't think a boy wants too much learning to spend fifteen-hundred a year.

Hardcastle. Learning, quotha! A mere composition of tricks and mischief.

Mrs. Hardcastle. Humor, my dear: nothing but humor. Come, Mr. Hardcastle, you must allow the boy a little humor.

Hardcastle. I'd sooner allow him an horse-pond. If burning the footmen's shoes, frighting the maids, and worrying the kittens, be humor, he has it. It was but yesterday he fastened my wig to the back of my chair, and when I went to make a bow I popped my bald head in Mrs. Frizzle's face.

Mrs. Hardcastle. And am I to blame? The poor boy was always too sickly to do any good. A school would be his death. When he comes to be a little stronger, who knows what a year or two's Latin may do for him?

Hardcastle. Latin for him! A cat and fiddle. No, no, the ale-house and the stable are the only schools he'll ever go to.

Mrs. Hardcastle. Well, we must not snub the poor boy now, for I believe we shan't have him long among us. Anybody that looks in his face may see he's consumptive.

Hardcastle. Ay, if growing too fat be one of the symptoms.

Mrs. Hardcastle. He coughs sometimes.

Hardcastle. Yes, when his liquor goes the wrong way.

Mrs. Hardcastle. I'm actually afraid of his lungs.

Hardcastle. And truly, so am I; for he sometimes whoops like a speaking trumpet—(TONY *hallooing behind the Scenes.*)—Oh, there he goes—A very consumptive figure, truly.

Enter TONY, *crossing the Stage.*

Mrs. Hardcastle. Tony, where are you going, my charmer? Won't you give papa and I a little of your company, lovee?

Tony. I'm in haste, mother, I cannot stay.

Mrs. Hardcastle. You shan't venture out this raw evening, my dear. You look most shockingly.

Tony. I can't stay, I tell you. The Three Pigeons expects me down every moment. There's some fun going forward.

Hardcastle. Ay; the ale-house, the old place. I thought so.

Mrs. Hardcastle. A low, paltry set of fellows.

Tony. Not so low neither. There's Dick Muggins the exciseman, Jack Slang the horse doctor, Little Aminadab that grinds the music box, and Tom Twist that spins the pewter platter.

Mrs. Hardcastle. Pray, my dear, disappoint them for one night at least.

Tony. As for disappointing *them*, I should not so much mind; but I can't abide to disappoint *myself*.

Mrs. Hardcastle. (*Detaining him.*) You shan't go.

Tony. I will, I tell you.

Mrs. Hardcastle. I say you shan't.

Tony. We'll see which is strongest, you or I.

Exit hauling her out.

HARDCASTLE, *solus.*

Hardcastle. Ay, there goes a pair that only spoil each other. But is not the whole age in a combination to drive sense and discretion out of doors? There's my pretty darling, Kate; the fashions of the times have almost infected her too. By living a year or two in town, she is as fond of gauze, and French frippery, as the best of them.

Enter MISS HARDCASTLE.

Hardcastle. Blessings on my pretty innocence! Dressed out as usual, my Kate. Goodness! What a quantity of superfluous silk hast thou got about thee, girl! I could never teach the fools of this age, that the indigent world could be clothed out of the trimmings of the vain.

Miss Hardcastle. You know our agreement, sir. You allow me the morning to receive and pay visits and to dress in my own manner; and in the evening, I put on my housewife's dress to please you.

Hardcastle. Well, remember, I insist on the terms of our agreement; and, by the bye, I believe I shall have occasion to try your obedience this very evening.

Miss Hardcastle. I protest, sir, I don't comprehend your meaning.

Hardcastle. Then to be plain with you, Kate, I expect the young gentleman I have chosen to be your husband from town this very day. I have his father's letter in which he informs me his son is set out and that he intends to follow himself shortly after.

Miss Hardcastle. Indeed! I wish I had known something of this before. Bless me, how shall I behave? It's a thousand to one I shan't like him. Our meeting will be so formal and so like a thing of business that I shall find no room for friendship or esteem.

Hardcastle. Depend upon it, child, I'll never control your choice; but Mr. Marlow, whom I have pitched upon, is the son of my old friend, Sir Charles Marlow, of whom you have heard me talk so often. The young gentleman has been bred a scholar, and is designed for an employment in the service of his country. I am told he's a man of excellent understanding.

Miss Hardcastle. Is he?

Hardcastle. Very generous.

Miss Hardcastle. I believe I shall like him.

Hardcastle. Young and brave.

Miss Hardcastle. I'm sure I shall like him.

Hardcastle. And very handsome.

Miss Hardcastle. My dear papa, say no more; (*kissing his hand.*) he's mine, I'll have him.

Hardcastle. And to crown all, Kate, he's one of the most bashful and reserved young fellows in all the world.

Miss Hardcastle. Eh! you have frozen me to death again. That word "reserved" has undone all the rest of his accomplishments. A reserved lover, it is said, always makes a suspicious husband.

Hardcastle. On the contrary, modesty seldom resides in a breast that is not enriched with nobler virtues. It was the very feature in his character that first struck me.

Miss Hardcastle. He must have more striking features to catch me, I promise you. However, if he be so young, so handsome, and so everything, as you mention, I believe he'll do still. I think I'll have him.

Hardcastle. Ay, Kate, but there is still an obstacle. It's more than an even wager he may not have *you.*

Miss Hardcastle. My dear Papa, why will you mortify one so?—Well, if he refuses, instead of breaking my heart at his indifference, I'll only break my glass for its flattery, set my cap to some newer fashion, and look out for some less difficult admirer.

Hardcastle. Bravely resolved! In the mean time I'll go prepare the servants for his reception; as we seldom see company they want as much training as a company of recruits, the first day's muster. *Exit.*

Miss Hardcastle, *sola.*

Miss Hardcastle. Lud, this news of Papa's put me all in a flutter. Young, handsome; these he put last; but I put them foremost. Sensible, good-natured; I like all that. But then reserved, and sheepish, that's much against him. Yet, can't he be cured of his timidity by being taught to be proud of his wife? Yes, and can't I—But I vow I'm disposing of the husband, before I have secured the lover.

Enter MISS NEVILLE.

Miss Hardcastle. I'm glad you're come, Neville, my dear. Tell me, Constance, how do I look this evening? Is there any thing whimsical about me? Is it one of my well looking days, child? Am I in face today?

Miss Neville. Perfectly, my dear. Yet now I look again—bless me!—sure no accident has happened among the canary birds or the gold-fishes. Has your brother or the cat been meddling? Or has the last novel been too moving?

Miss Hardcastle. No; nothing of all this. I have been threatened—I can scarce get it out—I have been threatened with a lover.

Miss Neville. And his name—

Miss Hardcastle. Is Marlow.

Miss Neville. Indeed!

Miss Hardcastle. The son of Sir Charles Marlow.

Miss Neville. As I live, the most intimate friend of Mr. Hastings, *my* admirer. They are never asunder. I believe you must have seen him when we lived in town.

Miss Hardcastle. Never.

Miss Neville. He's a very singular character, I assure you. Among women of reputation and virtue, he is the modestest man alive; but his acquaintance give him a very different character among creatures of another stamp: you understand me.

Miss Hardcastle. An odd character, indeed. I shall never be able to manage him. What shall I do? Pshaw, think no more of him, but trust to occurrences for success. But how goes on your own affair, my dear? has my mother been courting you for my brother Tony, as usual?

Miss Neville. I have just come from one of our agreeable *tête-à-têtes.* She has been saying a hundred tender things and setting off her pretty monster as the very pink of perfection.

Miss Hardcastle. And her partiality is such that she actually thinks him so. A fortune like yours is no small temptation. Besides, as she has the sole management of it, I'm not surprised to see her unwilling to let it go out of the family.

Miss Neville. A fortune like mine, which chiefly consists in jewels, is no such mighty temptation. But at any rate, if my dear Hastings be but constant, I make no doubt to be too hard for her at last. However, I let her suppose that I am in love with her son, and she never once dreams that my affections are fixed upon another.

Miss Hardcastle. My good brother holds out stoutly. I could almost love him for hating you so.

Miss Neville. It is a good natured creature at bottom, and I'm sure would wish to see me married to anybody but himself. But my aunt's bell rings for our afternoon's walk round the improvements. *Allons.* Courage is necessary as our affairs are critical.

Miss Hardcastle. Would it were bed time and all were well.
Exeunt.

SCENE II: *An Ale-house Room. Several shabby fellows with
    Punch and Tobacco.* TONY *at the head of the Table, a
    little higher than the rest: A mallet in his hand.*

Omnes. Hurrea, hurrea, hurrea, bravo!
First Fellow. Now, gentlemen, silence for a song. The
Squire is going to knock himself down for a song.
Omnes. Ay, a song, a song.
Tony. Then I'll sing you, gentlemen, a song I made upon
this ale-house, The Three Pigeons.

SONG

Let school-masters puzzle their brain
    With grammar, and nonsense, and learning;
Good liquor, I stoutly maintain,
    Gives genius a better discerning.
Let them brag of their Heathenish Gods,
    Their Lethes, their Styxes, and Stygians;
Their Quis, and their Quæs, and their Quods,
    They're all but a parcel of Pigeons.
                    Toroddle, toroddle, toroll!

When Methodist preachers come down,
    A-preaching that drinking is sinful,
I'll wager the rascals a crown,
    They always preach best with a skinful.
But when you come down with your pence,
    For a slice of their scurvy religion,
I'll leave it to all men of sense,
    But you, my good friend, are the pigeon.
                    Toroddle, toroddle, toroll!

Then come, put the jorum[4] about,
    And let us be merry and clever,
Our hearts and our liquors are stout,
    Here's the Three Jolly Pigeons for ever.
Let some cry up woodcock or hare,
    Your bustards, your ducks, and your widgeons;
But of all the birds in the air,
    Here's a health to the Three Jolly Pigeons.
                    Toroddle, toroddle, toroll!
Omnes. Bravo, bravo.
First Fellow. The squire has got spunk in him.

Second Fellow. I loves to hear him sing, bekeays he never gives us nothing that's *low*.

Third Fellow. O damn anything that's *low*, I cannot bear it.

Fourth Fellow. The genteel thing is the genteel thing at any time. If so be that a gentleman bees in a concatenation accordingly.

Third Fellow. I like the maxum of it, Master Muggins. What, though I am obligated to dance a bear, a man may be a gentleman for all that. May this be my poison if my bear ever dances but to the very genteelest of tunes. *Water Parted*, or the minuet in *Ariadne*.⁵

Second Fellow. What a pity it is the squire is not come to his own. It would be well for all the publicans within ten miles round of him.

Tony. Ecod, and so it would, Master Slang. I'd then show what it was to keep choice of company.

Second Fellow. Oh, he takes after his own father for that. To be sure old squire Lumpkin was the finest gentleman I ever set my eyes on. For winding the straight horn, or beating a thicket for a hare or a wench he never had his fellow. It was a saying in the place, that he kept the best horses, dogs and girls in the whole county.

Tony. Ecod, and when I'm of age I'll be no bastard, I promise you. I have been thinking of Bett Bouncer and the miller's grey mare to begin with. But come, my boys, drink about and be merry, for you pay no reckoning. Well, Stingo, what's the matter?

Enter LANDLORD.

Landlord. There be two gentlemen in a post-chaise at the door. They have lost their way upo' the forest; and they are talking something about Mr. Hardcastle.

Tony. As sure as can be, one of them must be the gentleman that's coming down to court my sister. Do they seem to be Londoners?

Landlord. I believe they may. They look woundily like Frenchmen.

Tony. Then desire them to step this way, and I'll set them right in a twinkling. (*Exit* LANDLORD.) Gentlemen, as they mayn't be good enough company for you, step down for a moment, and I'll be with you in the squeezing of a lemon.

Exeunt MOB.

TONY, *solus.*

Tony. Father-in-law has been calling me whelp and hound, this half year. Now if I pleased, I could be so revenged upon

the old grumbletonian. But then I'm afraid—afraid of what?
I shall soon be worth fifteen hundred a year, and let him
frighten me out of that if he can.

Enter LANDLORD, *conducting* MARLOW *and* HASTINGS.

Marlow. What a tedious, uncomfortable day have we had
of it! We were told it was but forty miles across the country,
and we have come above threescore.

Hastings. And all, Marlow, from that unaccountable reserve of yours that would not let us enquire more frequently
on the way.

Marlow. I own, Hastings, I am unwilling to lay myself
under an obligation to every one I meet; and often, stand
the chance of an unmannerly answer.

Hastings. At present, however, we are not likely to receive
any answer.

Tony. No offence, gentlemen. But I'm told you have been
enquiring for one Mr. Hardcastle in these parts. Do you
know what part of the country you are in?

Hastings. Not in the least, sir, but should thank you for
information.

Tony. Nor the way you came?

Hastings. No, sir; but if you can inform us—

Tony. Why, gentlemen, if you know neither the road you
are going, nor where you are, nor the road you came, the
first thing I have to inform you is, that—You have lost your
way.

Marlow. We wanted no ghost to tell us that.

Tony. Pray, gentlemen, may I be so bold as to ask the
place from whence you came?

Marlow. That's not necessary towards directing us where
we are to go.

Tony. No offence; but question for question is all fair, you
know. Pray, gentlemen, is not this the same Hardcastle a
cross-grained, old-fashioned, whimsical fellow, with an ugly
face, a daughter, and a pretty son?

Hastings. We have not seen the gentleman, but he has the
family you mention.

Tony. The daughter, a tall, trapesing, trolloping, talkative
maypole—The son, a pretty, well-bred, agreeable youth that
everybody is fond of.

Marlow. Our information differs in this. The daughter is
said to be well-bred and beautiful; the son, an awkward
booby, reared up and spoiled at his mother's apron-string.

Tony. He-he-hem—Then, gentlemen, all I have to tell you

is, that you won't reach Mr. Hardcastle's house this night, I believe.

Hastings. Unfortunate!

Tony. It's a damn'd long, dark, boggy, dirty, dangerous way. Stingo, tell the gentlemen the way to Mr. Hardcastle's; (*Winking upon the* LANDLORD.) Mr. Hardcastle's, of Quagmire Marsh, you understand me.

Landlord. Master Hardcastle's! Lack-a-daisy, my masters, you're come a deadly deal wrong! When you came to the bottom of the hill, you should have crossed down Squash-lane.

Marlow. Cross down Squash-lane!

Landlord. Then you were to keep straight forward, 'till you came to four roads.

Marlow. Come to where four roads meet!

Tony. Ay; but you must be sure to take only one of them.

Marlow. O sir, you're facetious.

Tony. Then keeping to the right, you are to go side-ways till you come upon Crack-skull Common. There you must look sharp for the track of the wheel and go forward 'till you come to farmer Murrain's barn. Coming to the farmer's barn, you are to turn to the right, and then to the left, and then to the right about again, till you find out the old mill—

Marlow. Zounds, man! we could as soon find out the longitude!

Hastings. What's to be done, Marlow?

Marlow. This house promises but a poor reception; though perhaps the Landlord can accommodate us.

Landlord. Alack, master, we have but one spare bed in the whole house.

Tony. And to my knowledge, that's taken up by three lodgers already. (*After a pause in which the rest seem disconcerted.*) I have hit it. Don't you think, Stingo, our landlady could accommodate the gentlemen by the fire-side, with —three chairs and a bolster?

Hastings. I hate sleeping by the fire-side.

Marlow. And I detest your three chairs and a bolster.

Tony. You do, do you?—then let me see—what—if you go on a mile further to the Buck's Head; the old Buck's Head on the hill, one of the best inns in the whole county?

Hastings. O ho! so we have escaped an adventure for this night.

Landlord. (*Apart to* TONY.) Sure, you ben't sending them to your father's as an inn, be you?

Tony. Mum, you fool you. Let *them* find that out. (*To them.*) You have only to keep on straight forward till you come to a large old house by the road side. You'll see a pair of large horns over the door. That's the sign. Drive up the yard and call stoutly about you.

Hastings. Sir, we are obliged to you. The servants can't miss the way?

Tony. No, no. But I tell you though, the landlord is rich and going to leave off business; so he wants to be thought a gentleman, saving your presence, he! he! he! He'll be for giving you his company, and, ecod, if you mind him, he'll persuade you that his mother was an alderman, and his aunt a justice of peace.

Landlord. A troublesome old blade, to be sure; but a keeps as good wines and beds as any in the whole country.

Marlow. Well, if he supplies us with these, we shall want no further connection. We are to turn to the right, did you say?

Tony. No, no; straight forward. I'll just step myself, and show you a piece of the way. (*To the* LANDLORD.) Mum.

Landlord. Ah, bless your heart, for a sweet, pleasant— damn'd mischievous son of a whore.   *Exeunt.*

ACT II

SCENE I: *An old-fashioned house.*

Enter HARDCASTLE, *followed by three or four awkward* SERVANTS.

Hardcastle. Well, I hope you're perfect in the table exercise I have been teaching you these three days. You all know your posts and your places and can show that you have been used to good company, without ever stirring from home.

Omnes. Ay, ay.

Hardcastle. When company comes, you are not to pop out and stare, and then run in again, like frightened rabbits in a warren.

Omnes. No, no.

Hardcastle. You, Diggory, whom I have taken from the barn, are to make a show at the side-table; and you, Roger, whom I have advanced from the plough, are to place yourself behind *my* chair. But you're not to stand so, with your hands in your pockets. Take your hands from your pockets, Roger; and from your head, you blockhead you. See how Diggory carries his hands. They're a little too stiff indeed, but that's no great matter.

Diggory. Ay, mind how I hold them. I learned to hold my

hands this way when I was upon drill for the militia. And so being upon drill—

Hardcastle. You must not be so talkative, Diggory. You must be all attention to the guests. You must hear us talk and not think of talking; you must see us drink and not think of drinking; you must see us eat and not think of eating.

Diggory. By the laws, your worship, that's perfectly unpossible. Whenever Diggory sees yeating going forward, ecod, he's always wishing for a mouthful himself.

Hardcastle. Blockhead! Is not a belly-full in the kitchen as good as a belly-full in the parlor? Stay your stomach with that reflection.

Diggory. Ecod, I thank your worship, I'll make a shift to stay my stomach with a slice of cold beef in the pantry.

Hardcastle. Diggory, you are too talkative. Then, if I happen to say a good thing, or tell a good story at table, you must not all burst out a-laughing, as if you made part of the company.

Diggory. Then, ecod, your worship must not tell the story of Ould Grouse in the gun-room: I can't help laughing at that—he! he! he!—for the soul of me. We have laughed at that these twenty years—ha! ha! ha!

Hardcastle. Ha! ha! ha! The story is a good one. Well, honest Diggory, you may laugh at that—but still remember to be attentive. Suppose one of the company should call for a glass of wine, how will you behave? A glass of wine, sir, if you please. (*To* DIGGORY.)—Eh, why don't you move?

Diggory. Ecod, your worship, I never have courage till I see the eatables and drinkables brought upo' the table, and then I'm as bauld as a lion.

Hardcastle. What, will nobody move?

First Servant. I'm not to leave this place.

Second Servant. I'm sure it's no pleace of mine.

Third Servant. Nor mine, for sartain.

Diggory. Wauns, and I'm sure it canna be mine.

Hardcastle. You numbskulls! and so while, like your betters, you are quarrelling for places, the guests must be starved. O you dunces! I find I must begin all over again.— But don't I hear a coach drive into the yard? To your posts, you blockheads. I'll go in the mean time and give my old friend's son a hearty reception at the gate.   Exit.

Diggory. By the elevens, my pleace is gone quite out of my head.

Roger. I know that my pleace is to be everywhere.

First Servant. Where the devil is mine?

Second Servant. My pleace is to be nowhere at all; and so I'ze go about my business.

Exeunt SERVANTS, *running about as if frighted, different ways.*

Enter SERVANT *with candles, showing in* MARLOW *and*
   HASTINGS.

Servant. Welcome, gentlemen, very welcome. This way.

Hastings. After the disappointments of the day, welcome
once more, Charles, to the comforts of a clean room and a
good fire. Upon my word, a very well-looking house; antique, but creditable.

Marlow. The usual fate of a large mansion. Having first
ruined the master by good housekeeping, it at last comes to
levy contributions as an inn.

Hastings. As you say, we passengers are to be taxed to pay
all these fineries. I have often seen a good sideboard, or a
marble chimney-piece, though not actually put in the bill, en-
flame a reckoning confoundedly.

Marlow. Travellers, George, must pay in all places. The
only difference is, that in good inns, you pay dearly for luxuries; in bad inns, you are fleeced and starved.

Hastings. You have lived pretty much among them. In
truth, I have been often surprised that you who have seen so
much of the world, with your natural good sense, and your
many opportunities, could never yet acquire a requisite
share of assurance.

Marlow. The Englishman's malady. But tell me, George,
where could I have learned that assurance you talk of? My
life has been chiefly spent in a college or an inn, in seclu-
sion from that lovely part of the creation that chiefly teach
men confidence. I don't know that I was ever familiarly acquainted with a single modest woman—except my mother—
But among females of another class, you know—

Hastings. Ay, among them you are impudent enough of all
conscience.

Marlow. They are of *us*, you know.

Hastings. But in the company of women of reputation I
never saw such an idiot, such a trembler; you look for all
the world as if you wanted an opportunity of stealing out of
the room.

Marlow. Why, man, that's because I *do* want to steal out of
the room. Faith, I have often formed a resolution to break
the ice, and rattle away at any rate. But I don't know how, a
single glance from a pair of fine eyes has totally overset my
resolution. An impudent fellow may counterfeit modesty, but
I'll be hanged if a modest man can ever counterfeit impudence.

Hastings. If you could but say half the fine things to them that I have heard you lavish upon the bar-maid of an inn, or even a college bed maker—

Marlow. Why, George, I can't say fine things to them. They freeze, they petrify me. They may talk of a comet, or a burning mountain, or some such bagatelle. But to me, a modest woman, dressed out in all her finery, is the most tremendous object of the whole creation.

Hastings. Ha! ha! ha! At this rate, man, how can you ever expect to marry!

Marlow. Never, unless, as among kings and princes, my bride were to be courted by proxy. If, indeed, like an Eastern bridegroom, one were to be introduced to a wife he never saw before, it might be endured. But to go through all the terrors of a formal courtship, together with the episode of aunts, grandmothers and cousins, and at last to blurt out the broad staring question of, *Madam, will you marry me?* No, no, that's a strain much above me, I assure you.

Hastings. I pity you. But how do you intend behaving to the lady you are come down to visit at the request of your father?

Marlow. As I behave to all other ladies. Bow very low. Answer yes, or no, to all her demands—But for the rest, I don't think I shall venture to look in her face, till I see my father's again.

Hastings. I'm surprised that one who is so warm a friend can be so cool a lover.

Marlow. To be explicit, my dear Hastings, my chief inducement down was to be instrumental in forwarding your happiness, not my own. Miss Neville loves you, the family don't know you; as my friend you are sure of a reception, and let honor do the rest.

Hastings. My dear Marlow! But I'll suppress the emotion. Were I a wretch, meanly seeking to carry off a fortune, you should be the last man in the world I would apply to for assistance. But Miss Neville's person is all I ask, and that is mine, both from her deceased father's consent and her own inclination.

Marlow. Happy man! You have talents and art to captivate any woman. I'm doomed to adore the sex, and yet to converse with the only part of it I despise. This stammer in my address and this awkward prepossessing visage of mine can never permit me to soar above the reach of a milliner's 'prentice, or one of the duchesses of Drury Lane.[6] Pshaw! this fellow here to interrupt us.

Enter HARDCASTLE.

Hardcastle. Gentlemen, once more you are heartily wel-

come. Which is Mr. Marlow? Sir, you're heartily welcome.
It's not my way, you see, to receive my friends with my
back to the fire. I like to give them a hearty reception in the
old style, at my gate. I like to see their horses and trunks
taken care of.

Marlow. (*Aside.*) He has got our names from the servants
already. (*To him.*) We approve your caution and hospitality,
sir. (*To* HASTINGS.) I have been thinking, George, of changing our travelling dresses in the morning. I am grown confoundedly ashamed of mine.

Hardcastle. I beg, Mr. Marlow, you'll use no ceremony in
this house.

Hastings. I fancy, Charles, you're right: the first blow is
half the battle. I intend opening the campaign with the white
and gold.

Mr. Hardcastle. Mr. Marlow—Mr. Hastings—gentlemen
—pray be under no constraint in this house. This is Liberty-
Hall, gentlemen. You may do just as you please here.

Marlow. Yet, George, if we open the campaign too fierce-
ly at first, we may want ammunition before it is over. I
think to reserve the embroidery to secure a retreat.

Hardcastle. Your talking of a retreat, Mr. Marlow, puts
me in mind of the Duke of Marlborough, when we went to
besiege Denain. He first summoned the garrison—

Marlow. Don't you think the *ventre d'or* waistcoat will
do with the plain brown?

Hardcastle. He first summoned the garrison, which might
consist of about five thousand men—

Hastings. I think not: brown and yellow mix but very
poorly.

Hardcastle. I say, gentlemen, as I was telling you, he summoned the garrison, which might consist of about five thousand men—

Marlow. The girls like finery.

Hardcastle. Which might consist of about five thousand
men, well appointed with stores, ammunition, and other im-
plements of war. "Now," says the Duke of Marlborough, to
George Brooks, that stood next to him—You must have
heard of George Brooks—"I'll pawn my Dukedom," says he,
"but I take that garrison without spilling a drop of blood."
So—

Marlow. What, my good friend, if you gave us a glass of
punch in the mean time; it would help us to carry on the
siege with vigor.

Hardcastle. Punch, sir! (*Aside.*) This is the most unaccountable kind of modesty I ever met with.

Government

Marlow. Yes, sir, punch. A glass of warm punch, after our journey, will be comfortable. This is Liberty-Hall, you know.

Hardcastle. Here's cup, sir.

Marlow. (*Aside.*) So this fellow, in his Liberty-Hall, will only let us have just what he pleases.

Hardcastle. (*Taking the Cup.*) I hope you'll find it to your mind. I have prepared it with my own hands, and I believe you'll own the ingredients are tolerable. Will you be so good as to pledge me, sir? Here, Mr. Marlow, here is to our better acquaintance.   (*Drinks.*)

Marlow. (*Aside.*) A very impudent fellow this! but he's a character and I'll humor him a little. Sir, my service to you.   (*Drinks.*)

Hastings. (*Aside.*) I see this fellow wants to give us his company, and forgets that he's an innkeeper, before he has learned to be a gentleman.

Marlow. From the excellence of your cup, my old friend, I suppose you have a good deal of business in this part of the country. Warm work, now and then, at elections, I suppose?

Hardcastle. No, sir, I have long given that work over. Since our betters have hit upon the expedient of electing each other, there's no business *for us that sell ale.*[7]

Hastings. So, then you have no turn for politics, I find.

Hardcastle. Not in the least. There was a time, indeed, I fretted myself about the mistakes of government, like other people; but finding myself every day grow more angry, and the government growing no better, I left it to mend itself. Since that, I no more trouble my head about Heyder Ally, or Ally Cawn, than about Ally Croaker.[8] Sir, my service to you.

Hastings. So that with eating above stairs, and drinking below, with receiving your friends within, and amusing them without you lead a good, pleasant, bustling life of it.

Hardcastle. I do stir about a great deal, that's certain. Half the differences of the parish are adjusted in this very parlor.

Marlow. (*After drinking.*) And you have an argument in your cup, old gentleman, better than any in Westminster Hall.

Hardcastle. Ay, young gentleman, that, and a little philosophy.

Marlow. (*Aside.*) Well, this is the first time I ever heard of an innkeeper's philosophy.

Hastings. So then, like an experienced general, you attack them on every quarter. If you find their reason manageable, you attack it with your philosophy; if you find they have no

reason, you attack them with this. Here's your health, my
philosopher.   (*Drinks.*)

Hardcastle. Good, very good, thank you; ha! ha! Your gen-
eralship puts me in mind of Prince Eugene, when he fought
the Turks at the battle of Belgrade. You shall hear——

Marlow. Instead of the battle of Belgrade, I believe it's almost time to talk about supper. What has your philosophy
got in the house for supper?

Hardcastle. For supper, sir! (*Aside.*) Was ever such a request to a man in his own house!

Marlow. Yes, sir, supper, sir; I begin to feel an appetite.
I shall make devilish work tonight in the larder, I promise
you.

Hardcastle. (*Aside.*) Such a brazen dog sure never my eyes
beheld. (*To him.*) Why really, sir, as for supper I can't well
tell. My Dorothy, and the cook-maid, settle these things between them. I leave these kind of things entirely to them.

Marlow. You do, do you?

Hardcastle. Entirely. By-the-bye, I believe they are in
actual consultation upon what's for supper this moment in
the kitchen.

Marlow. Then I beg they'll admit *me* as one of their privy
council. It's a way I have got. When I travel, I always choose
to regulate my own supper. Let the cook be called. No offence, I hope, sir.

Hardcastle. O no, sir, none in the least; yet I don't know
how: our Bridget, the cook maid, is not very communicative
upon these occasions. Should we send for her, she might
scold us all out of the house.

Hastings. Let's see your list of the larder then. I ask it as
a favor. I always match my appetite to my bill of fare.

Marlow. (*To* HARDCASTLE, *who looks at them with surprise.*) Sir, he's very right, and it's my way too.

Hardcastle. Sir, you have a right to command here. Here,
Roger, bring us the bill of fare for tonight's supper. I believe it's drawn out. Your manner, Mr. Hastings, puts me
in mind of my uncle, Colonel Wallop. It was a saying of his,
that no man was sure of his supper till he had eaten it.

Hastings. (*Aside.*) All upon the high ropes! His uncle a
Colonel! We shall soon hear of his mother being a justice of
peace. But let's hear the bill of fare.

Marlow. (*Perusing.*) What's here? For the first course; for
the second course; for the dessert. The devil, sir, do you
think we have brought down the whole Joiners Company, or
the Corporation of Bedford, to eat up such a supper? Two or
three little things, clean and comfortable, will do.

Hastings. But, let's hear it.

Marlow. (*Reading.*) For the first course, at the top, a pig and prune sauce.

Hastings. Damn your pig, I say.

Marlow. And damn your prune sauce, say I.

Hardcastle. And yet, gentlemen, to men that are hungry, pig with prune sauce is very good eating.

Marlow. At the bottom, a calve's tongue and brains.

Hastings. Let your brains be knocked out, my good sir; I don't like them.

Marlow. Or you may clap them on a plate by themselves. I do.

Hardcastle. (*Aside.*) Their impudence confounds me. (*To them.*) Gentlemen, you are my guests; make what alterations you please. Is there any thing else you wish to retrench or alter, gentlemen?

Marlow. Item: A pork pie, a boiled rabbit and sausages, a florentine, a shaking pudding, and a dish of tiff—taff—taffety cream![9]

Hastings. Confound your made dishes, I shall be as much at a loss in this house as at a green and yellow dinner at the French ambassador's table. I'm for plain eating.

Hardcastle. I'm sorry, gentlemen, that I have nothing you like, but if there be any thing you have a particular fancy to—

Marlow. Why, really, sir, your bill of fare is so exquisite that any one part of it is full as good as another. Send us what you please. So much for supper. And now to see that our beds are aired, and properly taken care of.

Hardcastle. I entreat you'll leave all that to me. You shall not stir a step.

Marlow. Leave that to you! I protest, sir, you must excuse me, I always look to these things myself.

Hardcastle. I must insist, sir, you'll make yourself easy on that head.

Marlow. You see I'm resolved on it. (*Aside.*) A very troublesome fellow this, as ever I met with.

Hardcastle. Well, sir, I'm resolved at least to attend you. (*Aside.*) This may be modern modesty, but I never saw any-thing look so like old-fashioned impudence.

Exeunt MARLOW *and* HARDCASTLE.

HASTINGS, *solus.*

Hastings. So I find this fellow's civilities begin to grow troublesome. But who can be angry at those assiduities which are meant to please him? Ha! what do I see? Miss Neville, by all that's happy!

Enter MISS NEVILLE.

Miss Neville. My dear Hastings! To what unexpected good fortune, to what accident am I to ascribe this happy meeting?

Hastings. Rather let me ask the same question, as I could never have hoped to meet my dearest Constance at an inn.

Miss Neville. An inn! sure you mistake! my aunt, my guardian, lives here. What could induce you to think this house an inn?

Hastings. My friend, Mr. Marlow, with whom I came down, and I, have been sent here as to an inn, I assure you. A young fellow whom we accidentally met at a house hard by directed us hither.

Miss Neville. Certainly it must be one of my hopeful cousin's tricks, of whom you have heard me talk so often, ha! ha! ha!

Hastings. He whom your aunt intends for you? He of whom I have such just apprehensions?

Miss Neville. You have nothing to fear from him, I assure you. You'd adore him if you knew how heartily he despises me. My aunt knows it too, and has undertaken to court me for him, and actually begins to think she has made a conquest.

Hastings. Thou dear dissembler! You must know, my Constance, I have just seized this happy opportunity of my friend's visit here to get admittance into the family. The horses that carried us down are now fatigued with their journey, but they'll soon be refreshed; and then, if my dearest girl will trust in her faithful Hastings, we shall soon be landed in France, where even among slaves the laws of marriage are respected.

Miss Neville. I have often told you, that though ready to obey you, I yet should leave my little fortune behind with reluctance. The greatest part of it was left me by my uncle, the India Director,[10] and chiefly consists in jewels. I have been for some time persuading my aunt to let me wear them. I fancy I'm very near succeeding. The instant they are put into my possession you shall find me ready to make them and myself yours.

Hastings. Perish the baubles! Your person is all I desire. In the meantime, my friend Marlow must not be let into his mistake. I know the strange reserve of his temper is such that if abruptly informed of it, he would instantly quit the house before our plan was ripe for execution.

Miss Neville. But how shall we keep him in the deception?

Miss Hardcastle is just returned from walking; what if we still continue to deceive him?—This, this way—

(*They confer.*)

Enter MARLOW.

Marlow. The assiduities of these good people tease me beyond bearing. My host seems to think it ill manners to leave me alone and so he claps not only himself but his old-fashioned wife on my back. They talk of coming to sup with us too; and then, I suppose, we are to run the gauntlet through all the rest of the family.—What have we got here!—

Hastings. My dear Charles! Let me congratulate you!—The most fortunate accident!—Who do you think is just alighted?

Marlow. Cannot guess.

Hastings. Our mistresses, boy, Miss Hardcastle and Miss Neville. Give me leave to introduce Miss Constance Neville to your acquaintance. Happening to dine in the neighborhood, they called, on their return, to take fresh horses, here. Miss Hardcastle has just stepped into the next room and will be back in an instant. Wasn't it lucky? eh!

Marlow. (*Aside.*) I have just been mortified enough of all conscience; and here comes something to complete my embarrassment.

Hastings. Well! but wasn't it the most fortunate thing in the world?

Marlow. Oh! yes. Very fortunate—a most joyful encounter —But our dresses, George, you know, are in disorder—What if we should postpone the happiness 'till tomorrow?—tomorrow at her own house—It will be every bit as convenient— And rather more respectful—Tomorrow let it be.

(*Offering to go.*)

Miss Neville. By no means, sir. Your ceremony will displease her. The disorder of your dress will show the ardor of your impatience. Besides, she knows you are in the house and will permit you to see her.

Marlow. Oh! the devil! how shall I support it? Hem! hem! Hastings, you must not go. You are to assist me, you know. I shall be confoundly ridiculous. Yet, hang it! I'll take courage. Hem!

Hastings. Pshaw, man! it's but the first plunge, and all's over. She's but a woman, you know.

Marlow. And of all women, she that I dread most to encounter!

Enter MISS HARDCASTLE *as returned from walking,* *a Bonnet, &c.*

Hastings. (Introducing them.) Miss Hardcastle, Mr. Marlow; I'm proud of bringing two persons of such merit together, that only want to know, to esteem each other.

Miss Hardcastle (Aside.) Now, for meeting my modest gentleman with a demure face and quite in his own manner. *(After a pause in which he appears very uneasy and disconcerted.)* I'm glad of your safe arrival, sir—I'm told you had some accidents by the way.

Marlow. Only a few, madam. Yes, we had some. Yes, madam, a good many accidents, but should be sorry— madam—or rather glad of any accidents—that are so agreeably concluded. Hem!

Hastings. (To him.) You never spoke better in your whole life. Keep it up, and I'll insure you the victory.

Miss Hardcastle. I'm afraid you flatter, sir. You that have seen so much of the finest company can find little entertainment in an obscure corner of the country.

Marlow. (Gathering courage.) I have lived, indeed, in the world, madam; but I have kept very little company. I have been but an observer upon life, madam, while others were enjoying it.

Miss Neville. But that, I am told, is the way to enjoy it at last.

Hastings. (To him.) Cicero never spoke better. Once more, and you are confirmed in assurance for ever.

Marlow. (To him.) Hem! Stand by me then, and when I'm down, throw in a word or two to set me up again.

Miss Hardcastle. An observer, like you, upon life were, I fear, disagreeably employed, since you must have had much more to censure than to approve.

Marlow. Pardon me, madam. I was always willing to be amused. The folly of most people is rather an object of mirth than uneasiness.

Hastings. (To him.) Bravo, bravo! Never spoke so well in your whole life. Well! Miss Hardcastle, I see that you and Mr. Marlow are going to be very good company. I believe our being here will but embarrass the interview.

Marlow. Not in the least, Mr. Hastings. We like your company of all things. *(To him.)* Zounds! George, sure you won't go? How can you leave us?

Hastings. Our presence will but spoil conversation, so we'll retire to the next room. *(To him.)* You don't consider, man, that we are to manage a little *tête-à-tête* of our own. *Exeunt.*

Miss Hardcastle. (After a pause.) But you have not been

wholly an observer, I presume, sir: The ladies I should hope have employed some part of your addresses.

Marlow. (*Relapsing into timidity.*) Pardon me, madam, I—I—I—as yet have studied—only—to—deserve them.

Miss Hardcastle. And that, some say, is the very worst way to obtain them.

Marlow. Perhaps so, madam. But I love to converse only with the more grave and sensible part of the sex.—But I'm afraid I grow tiresome.

Miss Hardcastle. Not at all, sir; there is nothing I like so much as grave conversation myself; I could hear it for ever. Indeed I have often been surprised how a man of *sentiment* could ever admire those light, airy pleasures, where nothing reaches the heart.

Marlow. It's—a disease—of the mind, madam. In the variety of tastes there must be some who, wanting a relish—for—um—a—um.

Miss Hardcastle. I understand you, sir. There must be some, who, wanting a relish for refined pleasures, pretend to despise what they are incapable of tasting.

Marlow. My meaning, madam, but infinitely better expressed. And I can't help observing—a—

Miss Hardcastle. (*Aside.*) Who could ever suppose this fellow impudent upon some occasions. (*To him.*) You were going to observe, sir—

Marlow. I was observing, madam—I protest, madam, I forget what I was going to observe.

Miss Hardcastle. (*Aside.*) I vow and so do I. (*To him.*) You were observing, sir, that in this age of hypocrisy—something about hypocrisy, sir.

Marlow. Yes, madam. In this age of hypocrisy there are few who upon strict enquiry do not—a—a—a—

Miss Hardcastle. I understand you perfectly, sir.

Marlow. (*Aside.*) Egad! and that's more than I do myself.

Miss Hardcastle. You mean that in this hypocritical age there are few that do not condemn in public what they practise in private and think they pay every debt to virtue when they praise it.

Marlow. True, madam; those who have most virtue in their mouths, have least of it in their bosoms. But I'm sure I tire you, Madam.

Miss Hardcastle. Not in the least, sir; there's something so agreeable and spirited in your manner, such life and force—pray, sir, go on.

Marlow. Yes, madam. I was saying—that there are some

occasions—when a total want of courage, madam, destroys all the—and puts us—upon a—a—a—

Miss Hardcastle. I agree with you entirely: a want of courage upon some occasions assumes the appearance of ignorance and betrays us when we most want to excel. I beg you'll proceed.

Marlow. Yes, madam. Morally speaking, madam—But I see Miss Neville expecting us in the next room. I would not intrude for the world.

Miss Hardcastle. I protest, sir, I never was more agreeably entertained in all my life. Pray go on.

Marlow. Yes, madam. I was—But she beckons us to join her. Madam, shall I do myself the honor to attend you?

Miss Hardcastle. Well then, I'll follow.

Marlow. (*Aside.*) This pretty, smooth dialogue has done for me.   *Exit.*

Miss Hardcastle, *sola.*

Miss Hardcastle. Ha! ha! ha! Was there ever such a sober, sentimental interview? I'm certain he scarce looked in my face the whole time. Yet the fellow, but for his unaccountable bashfulness, is pretty well, too. He has good sense, but then so buried in his fears that it fatigues one more than ignorance. If I could teach him a little confidence, it would be doing somebody that I know of a piece of service. But who is that somebody?—that, faith, is a question I can scarce answer.   *Exit.*

Enter Tony *and* Miss Neville, *followed by*
Mrs. Hardcastle *and* Hastings.

Tony. What do you follow me for, cousin Con? I wonder you're not ashamed to be so very engaging.

Miss Neville. I hope, cousin, one may speak to one's own relations and not be to blame.

Tony. Ay, but I know what sort of a relation you want to make me though; but it won't do. I tell you, cousin Con, it won't do; so I beg you'll keep your distance. I want no nearer relationship.

(*She follows coquetting him to the back scene.*)

Mrs. Hardcastle. Well! I vow Mr. Hastings, you are very entertaining. There's nothing in the world I love to talk of so much as London and the fashions, though I was never there myself.

Hastings. Never there! You amaze me! From your air and

manner, I concluded you had been bred all your life either at Ranelagh, St. James's, or Tower Wharf.[11]

Mrs. Hardcastle. O! Sir, you're only pleased to say so. We country persons can have no manner at all. I'm in love with the town and that serves to raise me above some of our neighbouring rustics; but who can have a manner that has never seen the Pantheon, the Grotto Gardens, the Borough, and such places where the Nobility chiefly resort? All I can do is to enjoy London at second-hand. I take care to know every *tête-á-tête* from the *Scandalous Magazine*,[12] and have all the fashions, as they come out, in a letter from the two Miss Rickets of Crooked Lane. Pray how do you like this head, Mr. Hastings?

Hastings. Extremely elegant and *degagée*, upon my word, Madam. Your *friseur* is a Frenchman, I suppose?

Mrs. Hardcastle. I protest I dressed it myself from a print in the *Ladies Memorandum Book* for the last year.

Hastings. Indeed. Such a head in a side-box, at the Playhouse, would draw as many gazers as my Lady May'ress at a City Ball.

Mrs. Hardcastle. I vow, since inoculation[13] began, there is no such thing to be seen as a plain woman; so one must dress a little particular or one may escape in the crowd.

Hastings. But that can never be your case madam, in any dress.

Mrs. Hardcastle. Yet, what signifies *my* dressing when I have such a piece of antiquity by my side as Mr. Hardcastle. All I can say will never argue down a single button from his clothes. I have often wanted him to throw off his great flaxen wig, and where he was bald, to plaster it over like my Lord Pately, with powder.

Hastings. You are right, Madam; for, as among the ladies, there are none ugly, so among the men there are none old.

Mrs. Hardcastle. But what do you think his answer was? Why, with his usual Gothic vivacity, he said I only wanted him to throw off his wig to convert it into a *tête* for my own wearing.

Hastings. Intolerable! At your age you may wear what you please, and it must become you.

Mrs. Hardcastle. Pray, Mr. Hastings, what do you take to be the most fashionable age about town?

Hastings. Some time ago, forty was all the mode; but I'm told the ladies intend to bring up fifty for the ensuing winter.

Mrs. Hardcastle. Seriously? Then I shall be too young for the fashion.

Hastings. No lady begins now to put on jewels 'till she's

past forty. For instance, Miss there, in a polite circle, would be considered as a child, as a mere maker of samplers.

Mrs. Hardcastle. And yet Mrs. Niece thinks herself as much a woman and is as fond of jewels as the oldest of us all.

Hastings. Your niece, is she? And that young gentleman, —a brother of yours, I should presume?

Mrs. Hardcastle. My son, sir. They are contracted to each other. Observe their little sports. They fall in and out ten times a day, as if they were man and wife already. (*To them.*) Well, Tony, child, what soft things are you saying to your cousin Constance this evening?

Tony. I have been saying no soft things; but that it's very hard to be followed about so. Ecod! I've not a place in the house now that's left to myself but the stable.

Mrs. Hardcastle. Never mind him, Con, my dear. He's in another story behind your back.

Miss Neville. There's something generous in my cousin's manner. He falls out before faces to be forgiven in private.

Tony. That's a damned confounded—crack.

Mrs. Hardcastle. Ah! he's a sly one. Don't you think they're like each other about the mouth, Mr. Hastings? The Blenkinsop mouth to a T. They're of a size too. Back to back, my pretties, that Mr. Hastings may see you. Come Tony.

Tony. You had as good not make me, I tell you.

(*Measuring.*)

Miss Neville. O lud! he has almost cracked my head.

Mrs. Hardcastle. O the monster! For shame, Tony. You a man, and behave so!

Tony. If I'm a man, let me have my fortin. Ecod! I'll not be made a fool of no longer.

Mrs. Hardcastle. Is this, ungrateful boy, all that I'm to get for the pains I have taken in your education? I that have rocked you in your cradle, and fed that pretty mouth with a spoon! Did not I work that waistcoat to make you genteel? Did not I prescribe for you every day and weep while the receipt was operating?

Tony. Ecod! you had reason to weep, for you have been dosing me ever since I was born. I have gone through every receipt in the complete huswife ten times over; and you have thoughts of coursing me through *Quincy*[14] next spring. But, ecod! I tell you, I'll not be made a fool of no longer.

Mrs. Hardcastle. Wasn't it all for your good, viper? Wasn't it all for your good?

Tony. I wish you'd let me and my good alone then. Snubbing this way when I'm in spirits. If I'm to have any good, let it come of itself; not to keep dinging it, dinging it into one so.

Mrs. Hardcastle. That's false; I never see you when you're in spirits. No, Tony, you then go to the alehouse or kennel. I'm never to be delighted with your agreeable, wild notes, unfeeling monster!

Tony. Ecod! Mamma, your own notes are the wildest of the two.

Mrs. Hardcastle. Was ever the like? But I see he wants to break my heart, I see he does.

Hastings. Dear Madam, permit me to lecture the young gentleman a little. I'm certain I can persuade him to his duty.

Mrs. Hardcastle. Well! I must retire. Come, Constance, my love. You see, Mr. Hastings, the wretchedness of my situation: Was ever poor woman so plagued with a dear, sweet, pretty, provoking, undutiful boy.

Exeunt MRS. HARDCASTLE *and* MISS NEVILLE.

HASTINGS, TONY.

Tony. (*Singing.*) *There was a young man riding by, and fain would have his will. Rang do didlo dee.* Don't mind her. Let her cry. It's the comfort of her heart. I have seen her and sister cry over a book for an hour together, and they said, they liked the book the better the more it made them cry.

Hastings. Then you're no friend to the ladies, I find, my pretty young gentleman?

Tony. That's as I find 'um.

Hastings. Not to her of your mother's choosing, I dare answer? And yet she appears to me a pretty, well-tempered girl.

Tony. That's because you don't know her as well as I. Ecod! I know every inch about her; and there's not a more bitter, cantankerous toad in all Christendom.

Hastings. (*Aside.*) Pretty encouragement this for a lover!

Tony. I have seen her since the height of that. She has as many tricks as a hare in a thicket, or a colt the first day's breaking.

Hastings. To me she appears sensible and silent!

Tony. Ay, before company. But when she's with her playmates, she's as loud as a hog in a gate.

Hastings. But there is a meek modesty about her that charms me.

Tony. Yes, but curb her never so little, she kicks up, and you're flung in a ditch.

Hastings. Well, but you must allow her a little beauty.—Yes, you must allow her some beauty.

Tony. Bandbox! She's all a made up thing, mun. Ah! could you but see Bett Bouncer of these parts, you might then talk of beauty. Ecod, she has two eyes as black as sloes, and cheeks as broad and red as a pulpit cushion. She'd make two of she.

Hastings. Well, what say you to a friend that would take this bitter bargain off your hands?

Tony. Anon.

Hastings. Would you thank him that would take Miss Neville and leave you to happiness and your dear Betsy?

Tony. Ay; but where is there such a friend, for who would take *her?*

Hastings. I am he. If you but assist me, I'll engage to whip her off to France and you shall never hear more of her.

Tony. Assist you! Ecod, I will, to the last drop of my blood. I'll clap a pair of horses to your chaise that shall trundle you off in a twinkling, and maybe get you a part of her fortin beside, in jewels, that you little dream of.

Hastings. My dear squire, this looks like a lad of spirit.

Tony. Come along then, and you shall see more of my spirit before you have done with me.   (*Singing.*)

> *We are the boys*
> *That fears no noise*
> *Where the thundering cannons roar. Exeunt.*

ACT III

SCENE I: *The house.*

Enter HARDCASTLE, *solus.*

Hardcastle. What could my old friend Sir Charles mean by recommending his son as the modestest young man in town? To me he appears the most impudent piece of brass that ever spoke with a tongue. He has taken possession of the easy chair by the fire-side already. He took off his boots in the parlor, and desired me to see them taken care of. I'm desirous to know how his impudence affects my daughter.— She will certainly be shocked at it.

Enter MISS HARDCASTLE, *plainly dressed.*

Hardcastle. Well, my Kate, I see you have changed your

dress as I bid you; and yet, I believe, there was no great occasion.

Miss Hardcastle. I find such a pleasure, sir, in obeying your commands, that I take care to observe them without ever debating their propriety.

Hardcastle. And yet, Kate, I sometimes give you some cause, particularly when I recommended my *modest* gentleman to you as a lover today.

Miss Hardcastle. You taught me to expect something extraordinary, and I find the original exceeds the description.

Hardcastle. I was never so surprised in my life! He has quite confounded all my faculties!

Miss Hardcastle. I never saw anything like it. And a man of the world too!

Hardcastle. Ay, he learned it all abroad,—what a fool was I, to think a young man could learn modesty by travelling. He might as soon learn wit at a masquerade.

Miss Hardcastle. It seems all natural to him.

Hardcastle. A good deal assisted by bad company and a French dancing-master.

Miss Hardcastle. Sure you mistake, papa! a French dancing-master could never have taught him that timid look,— that awkward address,—that bashful manner—

Hardcastle. Whose look? whose manner? child!

Miss Hardcastle. Mr. Marlow's: his *mauvaise honte*[15], his timidity struck me at the first sight.

Hardcastle. Then your first sight deceived you; for I think him one of the most brazen first sights that ever astonished my senses.

Miss Hardcastle. Sure, sir, you rally! I never saw any one so modest.

Hardcastle. And can you be serious! I never saw such a bouncing, swaggering puppy since I was born. Bully Dawson[16] was but a fool to him.

Miss Hardcastle. Surprising! He met me with a respectful bow, a stammering voice, and a look fixed on the ground.

Hardcastle. He met me with a loud voice, a lordly air, and a familiarity that made my blood freeze again.

Miss Hardcastle. He treated me with diffidence and respect; censured the manners of the age; admired the prudence of girls that never laughed; tired me with apologies for being tiresome; then left the room with a bow, and, "madam, I would not for the world detain you."

Hardcastle. He spoke to me as if he knew me all his life before. Asked twenty questions, and never waited for an answer. Interrupted my best remarks with some silly pun, and when I was in my best story of the Duke of Marlborough and Prince Eugene, he asked if I had not a good hand at making punch. Yes, Kate, he ask'd your father if he was a maker of punch!

Miss Hardcastle. One of us must certainly be mistaken.

Hardcastle. If he be what he has shown himself, I'm determined he shall never have my consent.

Miss Hardcastle. And if he be the sullen thing I take him, he shall never have mine.

Hardcastle. In one thing then we are agreed—to reject him.

Miss Hardcastle. Yes. But upon conditions. For if you should find him less impudent, and I more presuming; if you find him more respectful, and I more importunate—I don't know—the fellow is well enough for a man—Certainly we don't meet many such at a horse race in the country.

Hardcastle. If we should find him so—But that's impossible. The first appearance has done my business. I'm seldom deceived in that.

Miss Hardcastle. And yet there may be many good qualities under that first appearance.

Hardcastle. Ay, when a girl finds a fellow's outside to her taste, she then sets about guessing the rest of his furniture. With her, a smooth face stands for good sense, and a genteel figure for every virtue.

Miss Hardcastle. I hope, sir, a conversation begun with a compliment to my good sense won't end with a sneer at my understanding?

Hardcastle. Pardon me, Kate. But if young Mr. Brazen can find the art of reconciling contradictions, he may please us both, perhaps.

Miss Hardcastle. And as one of us must be mistaken, what if we go to make further discoveries?

Hardcastle. Agreed. But depend on't I'm in the right.

Miss Hardcastle. And depend on't I'm not much in the wrong.   *Exeunt.*

Enter TONY, *running in with a casket.*

Tony. Ecod! I have got them. Here they are. My Cousin Con's necklaces, bobs and all. My mother shan't cheat the poor souls out of their fortin neither. O! my genius, is that you?

Enter HASTINGS.

Hastings. My dear friend, how have you managed with

your mother? I hope you have amused her with pretending
love for your cousin, and that you are willing to be reconciled at last? Our horses will be refreshed in a short time,
and we shall soon be ready to set off.

Tony. And here's something to bear your charges by the
way. (*Giving the casket.*) Your sweetheart's jewels. Keep
them, and hang those, I say, that would rob you of one of
them.

Hastings. But how have you procured them from your
mother?

Tony. Ask me no questions, and I'll tell you no fibs. I
procured them by the rule of thumb. If I had not a key to
every drawer in mother's bureau, how could I go to the ale-
house so often as I do? An honest man may rob himself of
his own at any time.

Hastings. Thousands do it every day. But to be plain with
you; Miss Neville is endeavoring to procure them from her
aunt this very instant. If she succeeds, it will be the most
delicate way at least of obtaining them.

Tony. Well, keep them, till you know how it will be. But
I know how it will be well enough; she'd as soon part with
the only sound tooth in her head.

Hastings. But I dread the effects of her resentment, when
she finds she has lost them.

Tony. Never you mind her resentment; leave *me* to manage that. I don't value her resentment the bounce of a
cracker.[17] Zounds! here they are. Morrice.[18] Prance.

Exit HASTINGS.

TONY, MRS. HARDCASTLE, MISS NEVILLE.

Mrs. Hardcastle. Indeed, Constance, you amaze me. Such a
girl as you want jewels? It will be time enough for jewels,
my dear, twenty years hence, when your beauty begins to
want repairs.

Miss Neville. But what will repair beauty at forty, will
certainly improve it at twenty, madam.

Mrs. Hardcastle. Yours, my dear, can admit of none. That
natural blush is beyond a thousand ornaments. Besides, child,
jewels are quite out at present. Don't you see half the ladies
of our acquaintance, my Lady Kill-day-light, and Mrs.
Crump, and the rest of them, carry their jewels to town, and
bring nothing but Paste and Marcasites[19] back?

Miss Neville. But who knows, madam, but somebody that
shall be nameless would like me best with all my little
finery about me?

Mrs. Hardcastle. Consult your glass, my dear, and then

see if with such a pair of eyes you want any better sparklers. What do you think, Tony, my dear, does your Cousin Con want any jewels, in your eyes, to set off her beauty?

Tony. That's as thereafter may be.

Miss Neville. My dear aunt, if you knew how it would oblige me.

Mrs. Hardcastle. A parcel of old-fashioned rose and table-cut things.[20] They would make me look like the court of King Solomon at a puppet-show. Besides, I believe I can't readily come at them. They may be missing, for aught I know to the contrary.

Tony. (*Apart to* Mrs. Hardcastle.) Then why don't you tell her so at once, as she's so longing for them. Tell her they're lost. It's the only way to quiet her. Say they're lost, and call me to bear witness.

Mrs. Hardcastle. (*Apart to Tony.*) You know, my dear, I'm only keeping them for you. So if I say they're gone, you'll bear me witness, will you? He! he! he!

Tony. Never fear me. Ecod! I'll say I saw them taken out with my own eyes.

Miss Neville. I desire them but for a day, madam. Just to be permitted to show them as relics, and then they may be locked up again.

Mrs. Hardcastle. To be plain with you, my dear Constance, if I could find them, you should have them. They're missing, I assure you. Lost, for aught I know; but we must have patience wherever they are.

Miss Neville. I'll not believe it; this is but a shallow pretence to deny me. I know they're too valuable to be so slightly kept, and as you are to answer for the loss.

Mrs. Hardcastle. Don't be alarmed, Constance. If they be lost, I must restore an equivalent. But my son knows they are missing, and not to be found.

Tony. That I can bear witness to. They are missing and not to be found, I'll take my oath on't.

Mrs. Hardcastle. You must learn resignation, my dear; for though we lose our fortune, yet we should not lose our patience. See me, how calm I am.

Miss Neville. Ay, people are generally calm at the misfortunes of others.

Mrs. Hardcastle. Now, I wonder a girl of your good sense should waste a thought upon such trumpery. We shall soon find them; and, in the meantime, you shall make use of my garnets till your jewels be found.

Miss Neville. I detest garnets.

Mrs. Hardcastle. The most becoming things in the world to

set off a clear complexion. You have often seen how well they look upon me. You *shall* have them.   *Exit.*

Miss Neville. I dislike them of all things. You shan't stir. —Was ever any thing so provoking—to mislay my own jewels and force me to wear her trumpery.

Tony. Don't be a fool. If she gives you the garnets, take what you can get. The jewels are your own already. I have stolen them out of her bureau and she does not know it. Fly to your spark; he'll tell you more of the matter. Leave me to manage *her.*

Miss Neville. My dear cousin!

Tony. Vanish. She's here and has missed them already. (*Exit* Miss Neville.) Zounds! how she fidgets and spits about like a Catharine wheel.[21]

Enter Mrs. Hardcastle.

Mrs. Hardcastle. Confusion! thieves! robbers! We are cheated, plundered, broke open, undone.

Tony. What's the matter, what's the matter, mamma? I hope nothing has happened to any of the good family!

Mrs. Hardcastle. We are robbed. My bureau has been broke open, the jewels taken out, and I'm undone.

Tony. Oh, is that all? Ha! ha! ha! By the laws I never saw it better acted in my life. Ecod, I thought you was ruined in earnest, ha, ha, ha!

Mrs. Hardcastle. Why boy, I *am* ruined in earnest. My bureau has been broken open, and all taken away.

Tony. Stick to that; ha, ha, ha! stick to that. I'll bear witness, you know, call me to bear witness.

Mrs. Hardcastle. I tell you, Tony, by all that's precious, the jewels are gone, and I shall be ruined for ever.

Tony. Sure I know they're gone, and I am to say so.

Mrs. Hardcastle. My dearest Tony, but hear me. They're gone, I say.

Tony. By the laws, mamma, you make me for to laugh, ha! ha! I know who took them well enough, ha! ha! ha!

Mrs. Hardcastle. Was there ever such a blockhead, that can't tell the difference between jest and earnest. I tell you I'm not in jest, booby.

Tony. That's right, that's right. You must be in a bitter passion, and then nobody will suspect either of us. I'll bear witness that they are gone.

Mrs. Hardcastle. Was there ever such a cross-grained brute, that won't hear me! Can you bear witness that you're no better than a fool? Was ever poor woman so beset with fools on one hand, and thieves on the other?

Tony. I can bear witness to that.

Mrs. Hardcastle. Bear witness again, you blockhead you, and I'll turn you out of the room directly. My poor niece, what will become of *her!* Do you laugh, you unfeeling brute, as if you enjoyed my distress?

Tony. I can bear witness to that.

Mrs. Hardcastle. Do you insult me, monster? I'll teach you to vex your mother, I will.

Tony. I can bear witness to that.

He runs off, she follows him.

Enter MISS HARDCASTLE *and* MAID.

Miss Hardcastle. What an unaccountable creature is that brother of mine to send them to the house as an inn, ha! ha! I don't wonder at his impudence.

Maid. But what is more, madam, the young gentleman as you passed by in your present dress, asked me if you were the barmaid? He mistook you for the barmaid, madam.

Miss Hardcastle. Did he? Then as I live, I'm resolved to keep up the delusion. Tell me, Pimple, how do you like my present dress? Don't you think I look something like Cherry in the *Beaux' Stratagem?*[22]

Maid. It's the dress, madam, that every lady wears in the country, but when she visits, or receives company.

Miss Hardcastle. And are you sure he does not remember my face or person?

Maid. Certain of it.

Miss Hardcastle. I vow, I thought so; for though we spoke for some time together, yet his fears were such that he never once looked up during the interview. Indeed, if he had, my bonnet would have kept him from seeing me.

Maid. But what do you hope from keeping him in his mistake?

Miss Hardcastle. In the first place, I shall be *seen,* and that is no small advantage to a girl who brings her face to market. Then I shall perhaps make an acquaintance, and that's no small victory gained over one who never addresses any but the wildest of her sex. But my chief aim is to take my gentleman off his guard, and, like an invisible champion of romance, examine the giant's force before I offer to combat.

Maid. But are you sure you can act your part and disguise your voice, so that he may mistake that, as he has already mistaken your person?

Miss Hardcastle. Never fear me. I think I have got the true bar-cant.—Did your honor call?—Attend the Lion there. —Pipes and tobacco for the Angel.—The Lamb has been outrageous this half hour.[23]

Maid. It will do, madam. But he's here.   *Exit.*

Enter MARLOW.

Marlow. What a bawling in every part of the house. I have scarce a moment's repose. If I go to the best room, there I find my host and his story. If I fly to the gallery there we have my hostess with her curtsy down to the ground. I have at last got a moment to myself, and now for recollection.   (*Walks and muses.*)

Miss Hardcastle. Did you call, sir? Did your honor call?

Marlow. (*Musing.*) As for Miss Hardcastle, she's too grave and sentimental for me.

Miss Hardcastle. Did your honor call?

(*She still places herself before him, he turning away.*)

Marlow. No, child. (*Musing.*) Besides, from the glimpse I had of her, I think she squints.

Miss Hardcastle. I'm sure, sir, I heard the bell ring.

Marlow. No, no. (*Musing.*) I have pleased my father, however, by coming down, and I'll tomorrow please myself by returning.

                    (*Taking out his tablets,[24] and perusing.*)

Miss Hardcastle. Perhaps the other gentleman called, sir?

Marlow. I tell you, no.

Miss Hardcastle. I should be glad to know, sir. We have such a parcel of servants.

Marlow. No, no, I tell you. (*Looks full in her face.*) Yes, child, I think I did call. I wanted—I wanted—I vow, child, you are vastly handsome.

Miss Hardcastle. O la, sir, you'll make one ashamed.

Marlow. Never saw a more sprightly, malicious eye. Yes, yes, my dear, I did call. Have you got any of your—a—what d'ye call it in the house?

Miss Hardcastle. No, sir, we have been out of that these ten days.

Marlow. One may call in this house, I find, to very little purpose. Suppose I should call for a taste, just by way of trial, of the nectar of your lips; perhaps I might be disappointed in that too.

Miss Hardcastle. Nectar! nectar! That's a liquor there's no call for in these parts. French, I suppose. We keep no French wines here, sir.

Marlow. Of true English growth, I assure you.

Miss Hardcastle. Then it's odd I should not know it. We brew all sorts of wines in this house, and I have lived here these eighteen years.

Marlow. Eighteen years! Why one would think, child, you kept the bar before you were born. How old are you?

Miss Hardcastle. O! Sir, I must not tell my age. They say women and music should never be dated.

Marlow. To guess at this distance, you can't be much above forty. (*Approaching.*) Yet nearer, I don't think so much. (*Approaching.*) By coming close to some women, they look younger still; but when we come very close indeed—

(*Attempting to kiss her.*)

Miss Hardcastle. Pray, sir, keep your distance. One would think you wanted to know one's age as they do horses, by mark of mouth.

Marlow. I protest, child, you use me extremely ill. If you keep me at this distance how is it possible you and I can be ever acquainted?

Miss Hardcastle. And who wants to be acquainted with you? I want no such acquaintance, not I. I'm sure you did not treat Miss Hardcastle that was here awhile ago in this obstropalous manner. I'll warrant me, before her you looked dashed, and kept bowing to the ground, and talked for all the world as if you was before a justice of peace.

Marlow. (*Aside.*) Egad! she has hit it, sure enough. (*To her.*) In awe of her, child? Ha! ha! ha! A mere, awkward, squinting thing? no, no! I find you don't know me. I laughed and rallied her a little; but I was unwilling to be too severe. No, I could not be too severe, curse me!

Miss Hardcastle. Oh! then, sir, you are a favorite, I find, among the ladies?

Marlow. Yes, my dear, a great favorite. And yet, hang me, I don't see what they find in me to follow. At the Ladies Club in town, I'm called their agreeable Rattle. Rattle, child, is not my real name, but one I'm known by. My name is Solomons. Mr. Solomons, my dear, at your service.

(*Offering to salute her.*)

Miss Hardcastle. Hold, sir; you are introducing me to your club, not to yourself. And you're so great a favorite there, you say?

Marlow. Yes, my dear. There's Mrs. Mantrap, Lady Betty Blackleg, the Countess of Sligo, Mrs. Langhorns, old Miss Biddy Buckskin, and your humble servant, keep up the spirit of the place.

Miss Hardcastle. Then it's a very merry place, I suppose?

Marlow. Yes, as merry as cards, suppers, wine, and old women can make us.

Miss Hardcastle. And their agreeable Rattle, ha! ha! ha!

Marlow. (*Aside.*) Egad! I don't quite like this chit. She looks knowing, methinks. You laugh, child!

Miss Hardcastle. I can't but laugh to think what time they all have for minding their work or their family.

Marlow. (*Aside.*) All's well; she don't laugh at me. (*To her.*) Do *you* ever work, child?

Miss Hardcastle. Ay, sure. There's not a screen or a quilt in the whole house but what can bear witness to that.

Marlow. Odso! Then you must show me your embroidery. I embroider and draw patterns myself a little. If you want a judge of your work you must apply to me.

(*Seizing her hand.*)

Miss Hardcastle. Ay, but the colors don't look well by candlelight. You shall see all in the morning   (*Struggling.*)

Marlow. And why not now, my angel? Such beauty fires beyond the power of resistance.—Pshaw! the father here! My old luck: I never nicked seven that I did not throw ames ace three times following.[25]   *Exit.*

Enter HARDCASTLE, *who stands in surprise.*

Hardcastle. So, madam. So I find *this* is your *modest* lover. This is your humble admirer that kept his eyes fixed on the ground, and only adored at humble distance. Kate, Kate, art thou not ashamed to deceive your father so?

Miss Hardcastle. Never trust me, dear papa, but he's still the modest man I first took him for; you'll be convinced of it as well as I.

Hardcastle. By the hand of my body, I believe his impudence is infectious! Didn't I see him seize your hand? Didn't I see him haul you about like a milkmaid? and now you talk of his respect and his modesty, forsooth!

Miss Hardcastle. But if I shortly convince you of his modesty, that he has only the faults that will pass off with time, and the virtues that will improve with age, I hope you'll forgive him.

Hardcastle. The girl would actually make one run mad! I tell you I'll not be convinced. I am convinced. He has scarcely been three hours in the house, and he has already encroached on all my prerogatives. You may like his impudence, and call it modesty. But my son-in-law, madam, must have very different qualifications.

Miss Hardcastle. Sir, I ask but this night to convince you.

Hardcastle. You shall not have half the time, for I have thoughts of turning him out this very hour.

Miss Hardcastle. Give me that hour then, and I hope to satisfy you.

Hardcastle. Well, an hour let it be then. But I'll have no trifling with your father. All fair and open, do you mind me?

Miss Hardcastle. I hope, sir, you have ever found that I considered your commands as my pride; for your kindness is such that my duty as yet has been inclination.   *Exeunt*.

ACT IV

SCENE I: *The house*.

Enter HASTINGS *and* MISS NEVILLE.

Hastings. You surprise me! Sir Charles Marlow expected here this night? Where have you had your information?

Miss Neville. You may depend upon it. I just saw his letter to Mr. Hardcastle, in which he tells him he intends setting out a few hours after his son.

Hastings. Then, my Constance, all must be completed before he arrives. He knows me; and should he find me here, would discover my name and perhaps my designs to the rest of the family.

Miss Neville. The jewels, I hope, are safe.

Hastings. Yes, yes. I have sent them to Marlow, who keeps the keys of our baggage. In the meantime, I'll go to prepare matters for our elopement. I have had the squire's promise of a fresh pair of horses; and, if I should not see him again will write him further directions.   *Exit*.

Miss Neville. Well! success attend you. In the meantime, I'll go amuse my aunt with the old pretence of a violent passion for my cousin.   *Exit*.

Enter MARLOW, *followed by a* SERVANT.

Marlow. I wonder what Hastings could mean by sending me so valuable a thing as a casket to keep for him, when he knows the only place I have is the seat of a post-coach at an inn door. Have you deposited the casket with the landlady, as I ordered you? Have you put it into her own hands?

Servant. Yes, your honor.

Marlow. She said she'd keep it safe, did she?

Servant. Yes, she said she'd keep it safe enough; she asked me how I came by it? and she said she had a great mind to make me give an account of myself.   *Exit*.

Marlow. Ha! ha! ha! They're safe, however. What an unaccountable set of beings have we got amongst! This little barmaid, though, runs in my head most strangely and drives out the absurdities of all the rest of the family. She's mine, she must be mine, or I'm greatly mistaken.

Enter HASTINGS.

Hastings. Bless me! I quite forgot to tell her that I intended to prepare at the bottom of the garden. Marlow here, and in spirits too!

Marlow. Give me joy, George! Crown me, shadow me with laurels! Well, George, after all, we modest fellows don't want for success among the women.

Hastings. Some women, you mean. But what success has your honor's modesty been crowned with now, that it grows so insolent upon us?

Marlow. Didn't you see the tempting, brisk, lovely, little thing that runs about the house with a bunch of keys to its girdle?

Hastings. Well! and what then?

Marlow. She's mine, you rogue you. Such fire, such motion, such eyes, such lips—but, egad! she would not let me kiss them, though.

Hastings. But are you so sure, so very sure of her?

Marlow. Why man, she talked of showing me her work above-stairs, and I am to improve the pattern.

Hastings. But how can *you*, Charles, go about to rob a woman of her honor?

Marlow. Pshaw! pshaw! we all know the honor of the barmaid of an inn. I don't intend to *rob* her, take my word for it; there's nothing in this house I shan't honestly *pay* for.

Hastings. I believe the girl has virtue.

Marlow. And if she has, I should be the last man in the world that would attempt to corrupt it.

Hastings. You have taken care, I hope, of the casket I sent you to lock up? It's in safety?

Marlow. Yes, yes. It's safe enough. I have taken care of it. But how could you think the seat of a post-coach at an inn door a place of safety? Ah! numbskull! I have taken better precautions for you than you did for yourself.—I have—

Hastings. What!

Marlow. I have sent it to the landlady to keep for you.

Hastings. To the landlady!

Marlow. The landlady.

Hastings. You did!

Marlow. I did. She's to be answerable for its forthcoming, you know.

Hastings. Yes, she'll bring it forth, with a witness.

Marlow. Wasn't I right? I believe you'll allow that I acted prudently upon this occasion?

Hastings. (*Aside.*) He must not see my uneasiness.

Marlow. You seem a little disconcerted though, methinks. Sure nothing has happened?

Hastings. No, nothing. Never was in better spirits in all my life. And so you left it with the landlady, who, no doubt, very readily undertook the charge?

Marlow. Rather too readily. For she not only kept the casket; but, through her great precaution, was going to keep the messenger too. Ha! ha! ha!

Hastings. He! he! he! They're safe, however.

Marlow. As a guinea in a miser's purse.

Hastings. (*Aside.*) So now all hopes of fortune are at an end, and we must set off without it. (*To him.*) Well, Charles, I'll leave you to your meditations on the pretty barmaid, and, he! he! he! may you be as successful for yourself as you have been for me.   *Exit.*

Marlow. Thank ye, George! I ask no more! Ha! ha! ha!

Enter HARDCASTLE.

Hardcastle. I no longer know my own house. It's turned all topsey-turvey. His servants have got drunk already. I'll bear it no longer, and yet, from my respect for his father, I'll be calm. (*To him.*) Mr. Marlow, your servant. I'm your very humble servant.   (*Bowing low.*)

Marlow. Sir, your humble servant. (*Aside.*) What's to be the wonder now?

Hardcastle. I believe, sir, you must be sensible, sir, that no man alive ought to be more welcome than your father's son, sir. I hope you think so?

Marlow. I do from my soul, sir. I don't want much intreaty. I generally make my father's son welcome wherever he goes.

Hardcastle. I believe you do, from my soul, sir. But though I say nothing to your own conduct, that of your servants is insufferable. Their manner of drinking is setting a very bad example in this house, I assure you.

Marlow. I protest, my very good sir, that's no fault of mine. If they don't drink as they ought, *they* are to blame. I ordered them not to spare the cellar. I did, I assure you. (*To the side scene.*) Here, let one of my servants come up. (*To him.*) My positive directions were, that as I did not drink myself, they should make up for my deficiencies below.

Hardcastle. Then they had your orders for what they do! I'm satisfied!

Marlow. They had, I assure you. You shall hear from one of themselves.

Enter SERVANT *drunk.*

Marlow. You, Jeremy! Come forward, sirrah! What were my orders? Were you not told to drink freely, and call for what you thought fit, for the good of the house?

Hardcastle. (*Aside.*) I begin to lose my patience.

Jeremy. Please your honor, liberty and Fleet Street for ever! Though I'm but a servant, I'm as good as another man. I'll drink for no man before supper, sir, dammy! Good liquor will sit upon a good supper, but a good supper will not sit upon—*hiccup*—upon my conscience, sir.   *Exit.*

Marlow. You see, my old friend, the fellow is as drunk as he can possibly be. I don't know what you'd have more, unless you'd have the poor devil soused in a beer-barrel.

Hardcastle. Zounds! He'll drive me distracted if I contain myself any longer.—Mr. Marlow, sir; I have submitted to your insolence for more than four hours, and I see no likelihood of its coming to an end. I'm now resolved to be master here, sir, and I desire that you and your drunken pack may leave my house directly.

Marlow. Leave your house!—Sure you jest, my good friend! What, when I'm doing what I can to please you!

Hardcastle. I tell you, sir, you don't please me; so I desire you'll leave my house.

Marlow. Sure you cannot be serious? At this time o'night, and such a night? You only mean to banter me?

Hardcastle. I tell you, sir, I'm serious; and, now that my passions are roused, I say this house is mine, sir; this house is mine, and I command you to leave it directly.

Marlow. Ha! ha! ha! A puddle in a storm. I shan't stir a step, I assure you. (*In a serious tone.*) This, your house, fellow! It's my house. This is my house. Mine, while I choose to stay. What right have you to bid me leave this house, sir? I never met with such impudence, curse me, never in my whole life before.

Hardcastle. Nor I, confound me if ever I did. To come to my house, to call for what he likes, to turn me out of my own chair, to insult the family, to order his servants to get drunk, and then to tell me *This house is mine, sir.* By all that's impudent, it makes me laugh. Ha! ha! ha! Pray, sir, (*bantering*) as you take the house, what think you of taking the rest of the furniture? There's a pair of silver candlesticks, and there's a fire-screen, and here's a pair of brazen-nosed bellows, perhaps you may take a fancy to them?

Marlow. Bring me your bill, sir, bring me your bill, and let's make no more words about it.

Hardcastle. There are a set of prints too. What think you of *The Rake's Progress*²⁶ for your own apartment?

Marlow. Bring me your bill, I say; and I'll leave you and your infernal house directly.

Hardcastle. Then there's a mahogany table, that you may see your own face in.

Marlow. My bill, I say.

Hardcastle. I had forgot the great chair, for your own particular slumbers after a hearty meal.

Marlow. Zounds! bring me my bill, I say, and let's hear no more on't.

Hardcastle. Young man, young man, from your father's letter to me, I was taught to expect a well-bred, modest man, as a visitor here, but now I find him no better than a coxcomb and a bully; but he will be down here presently, and shall hear more of it.   *Exit.*

Marlow. How's this! Sure I have not mistaken the house? Everything looks like an inn. The servants cry, *Coming.* The attendance is awkward; the barmaid, too, to attend us. But she's here, and will further inform me. Whither so fast, child? A word with you.

Enter MISS HARDCASTLE.

Miss Hardcastle. Let it be short then. I'm in a hurry. (*Aside.*) I believe he begins to find out his mistake, but it's too soon quite to undeceive him.

Marlow. Pray, child, answer me one question. What are you, and what may your business in this house be?

Miss Hardcastle. A relation of the family, sir.

Marlow. What! A poor relation?

Miss Hardcastle. Yes, sir. A poor relation appointed to keep the keys, and to see that the guests want nothing in my power to give them.

Marlow. That is, you act as the barmaid of this inn.

Miss Hardcastle. Inn! O law—what brought that in your head? One of the best families in the county keep an inn! Ha, ha, ha, old Mr. Hardcastle's house an inn?

Marlow. Mr. Hardcastle's house? Is this house Mr. Hardcastle's house, child?

Miss Hardcastle. Ay, sure. Whose else should it be?

Marlow. So then all's out, and I have been damnably imposed on. Oh, confound my stupid head, I shall be laughed at over the whole town. I shall be stuck up in *caricatura* in all the printshops. The Dullissimo Maccaroni.[27] To mistake this house of all others for an inn, and my father's old friend for an inn-keeper. What a swaggering puppy must he take me for. What a silly puppy do I find myself. There again, may I be hanged, my dear, but I mistook you for the barmaid.

Miss Hardcastle. Dear me! dear me! I'm sure there's nothing in my *behavior* to put me upon a level with one of that stamp.

Marlow. Nothing, my dear, nothing. But I was in for a list of blunders, and could not help making you a subscriber. My stupidity saw everything the wrong way. I mistook your assiduity for assurance and your simplicity for allurement. But it's over—This house I no more show *my* face in.

Miss Hardcastle. I hope, sir, I have done nothing to disoblige you. I'm sure I should be sorry to affront any gentleman who has been so polite, and said so many civil things to me. I'm sure I should be sorry (*pretending to cry*) if he left the family upon my account. I'm sure I should be sorry, if people said anything amiss, since I have no fortune but my character.

Marlow. (*Aside.*) By heaven, she weeps. This is the first mark of tenderness I ever had from a modest woman, and it touches me. (*To her.*) Excuse me, my lovely girl, you are the only part of the family I leave with reluctance. But to be plain with you, the difference of our birth, fortune, and education make an honorable connection impossible; and I can never harbor a thought of seducing simplicity that trusted in my honor, or bringing ruin upon one, whose only fault was being too lovely.

Miss Hardcastle. (*Aside.*) Generous man! I now begin to admire him. (*To him.*) But I'm sure my family is as good as Miss Hardcastle's, and though I'm poor, that's no great misfortune to a contented mind, and, until this moment, I never thought that it was bad to want fortune.

Marlow. And why now, my pretty simplicity?

Miss Hardcastle. Because it puts me at a distance from one that if I had a thousand pound I would give it all to.

Marlow. (*Aside.*) This simplicity bewitches me, so that if I stay I'm undone. I must make one bold effort, and leave her. (*To her.*) Your partiality in my favor, my dear, touches me most sensibly, and were I to live for myself alone, I could easily fix my choice. But I owe too much to the opinion of the world, too much to the authority of a father, so that—I can scarcely speak it—it affects me. Farewell. *Exit.*

Miss Hardcastle. I never knew half his merit till now. He shall not go, if I have power or art to detain him. I'll still preserve the character in which I stooped to conquer, but will undeceive my papa, who, perhaps, may laugh him out of his resolution.
                                                                Exit.

Enter TONY, MISS NEVILLE.

Tony. Ay, you may steal for yourselves the next time. I have done my duty. She has got the jewels again, that's a sure thing; but she believes it was all a mistake of the servants.

Miss Neville. But, my dear cousin, sure you won't forsake us in this distress. If she in the least suspects that I am going off, I shall certainly be locked up or sent to my Aunt Pedigree's, which is ten times worse.

Tony. To be sure, aunts of all kinds are damned bad things. But what can I do? I have got you a pair of horses that will fly like Whistlejacket, and I'm sure you can't say but I have courted you nicely before her face. Here she comes; we must court a bit or two more, for fear she should suspect us.

                    (*They retire, and seem to fondle.*)

Enter MRS. HARDCASTLE.

Mrs. Hardcastle. Well, I was greatly fluttered, to be sure. But my son tells me it was all a mistake of the servants. I shan't be easy, however, until they are fairly married, and then let her keep her own fortune. But what do I see! Fondling together, as I'm alive. I never saw Tony so sprightly before. Ah! have I caught you, my pretty doves? What, billing, exchanging stolen glances, and broken murmurs. Ah!

Tony. As for murmurs, mother, we grumble a little now and then, to be sure. But there's no love lost between us.

Mrs. Hardcastle. A mere sprinkling, Tony, upon the flame, only to make it burn brighter.

Miss Neville. Cousin Tony promises to give us more of his company at home. Indeed, he shan't leave us any more. It won't leave us, cousin Tony, will it?

Tony. Oh! it's a pretty creature. No, I'd soon leave my horse in a pound, than leave you when you smile upon one so. Your laugh makes you so becoming.

Miss Neville. Agreeable cousin! Who can help admiring that natural humor, that pleasant, broad, red, thoughtless (*patting his cheek*) ah! it's a bold face.

Mrs. Hardcastle. Pretty innocence!

Tony. I'm sure I always loved cousin Con's hazel eyes, and her pretty long fingers, that she twists this way and that over the haspicholls,[28] like a parcel of bobbins.

Mrs. Hardcastle. Ah, he would charm the bird from the tree. I was never so happy before. My boy takes after his father, poor Mr. Lumpkin, exactly. The jewels, my dear Con, shall be yours incontinently. You shall have them. Isn't he a sweet boy, my dear? You shall be married tomorrow, and we'll put off the rest of his education, like Dr. Drowsy's sermons, to a fitter opportunity.

Enter DIGGORY.

Diggory. Where's the squire? I have got a letter for your worship.

Tony. Give it to my mama. She reads all my letters first.

Diggory. I had orders to deliver it into your own hands.

Tony. Who does it come from?

Diggory. Your worship mun ask that o' the letter itself.

Exit.

Tony. I could wish to know, though.

(*Turning the letter, and gazing on it.*)

Miss Neville. (*Aside.*) Undone, undone. A letter to him from Hastings. I know the hand. If my aunt sees it, we are ruined for ever. I'll keep her employed a little if I can. (*To* MRS. HARDCASTLE.) But I have not told you, Madam, of my cousin's smart answer just now to Mr. Marlow. We so laughed—You must know, Madam—this way a little, for he must not hear us. (*They confer.*)

Tony. (*Still gazing.*) A damned cramp piece of penmanship, as ever I saw in my life. I can read your print-hand very well. But here there are such handles, and shanks, and dashes, that one can scarce tell the head from the tail. *To Anthony Lumpkin, Esquire.* It's very odd, I can read the outside of my letters, where my own name is, well enough. But when I come to open it, it's all—buzz. That's hard, very hard; for the inside of the letter is always the cream of the correspondence.

Mrs. Hardcastle. Ha! ha! ha! Very well, very well! And so my son was too hard for the philosopher.

Miss Neville. Yes, madam; but you must hear the rest, madam. A little more this way, or he may hear us. You'll hear how he puzzled him again.

Mrs. Hardcastle. He seems strangely puzzled now himself, methinks.

Tony. (*Still gazing.*) A damned up-and-down hand, as if it was disguised in liquor. (*Reading.*) *Dear Sir.* Ay, that's that.

Then there's an *M*, and a *T*, and an *S*, but whether the next be an *izzard* or an *R*, confound me, I cannot tell.

Mrs. Hardcastle. What's that, my dear? Can I give you any assistance?

Miss Neville. Pray, aunt, let me read it. Nobody reads a cramp hand better than I. (*Twitching the letter from her.*) Do you know who it is from?

Tony. Can't tell, except from Dick Ginger the feeder.

Miss Neville. Ay, so it is. (*Pretending to read.*) Dear Squire, Hoping that you're in health, as I am at this present. The gentlemen of the Shake-bag club has cut the gentlemen of Goose-green quite out of feather. The odds—um—odd battle —um—long fighting—um, here, here, it's all about cocks, and fighting; it's of no consequence; here, put it up, put it up. (*Thrusting the crumpled letter upon him.*)

Tony. But I tell you, miss, it's of all the consequence in the world. I would not lose the rest of it for a guinea. Here, mother, do you make it out. Of no consequence!

(*Giving* Mrs. Hardcastle *the letter.*)

Mrs. Hardcastle. How's this! (*Reads.*) "Dear Squire, I'm now waiting for Miss Neville with a post-chaise and pair at the bottom of the garden, but I find my horses yet unable to perform the journey. I expect you'll assist us with a pair of fresh horses, as you promised. Dispatch is necessary, as the *hag*, (ay, the hag) your mother, will otherwise suspect us. Yours, Hastings." Grant me patience. I shall run distracted! My rage chokes me!

Miss Neville. I hope, madam, you'll suspend your resentment for a few moments, and not impute to me any impertinence, or sinister design that belongs to another.

Mrs. Hardcastle. (*Curtsying very low.*) Fine spoken, madam; you are most miraculously polite and engaging and quite the very pink of courtesy and circumspection, madam. (*Changing her tone.*) And you, you great ill-fashioned oaf, with scarce sense enough to keep your mouth shut. Were you too joined against me? But I'll defeat all your plots in a moment. As for you, madam, since you have got a pair of fresh horses ready, it would be cruel to disappoint them. So, if you please, instead of running away with your spark, prepare, this very moment, to run off with *me*. Your old Aunt Pedigree will keep you secure, I'll warrant me. You too, sir, may mount your horse, and guard us upon the way. Here, Thomas, Roger, Diggory! I'll show you, that I wish you better than you do yourselves.   *Exit.*

Miss Neville. So now I'm completely ruined.

Tony. Ay, that's a sure thing.

Miss Neville. What better could be expected from being

connected with such a stupid fool, and after all the nods and
signs I made him.

Tony. By the laws, miss, it was your own cleverness and
not my stupidity that did your business. You were so nice
and so busy with your Shake-bags and Goose-greens, that I
thought you could never be making believe.

Enter HASTINGS.

Hastings. So, sir, I find by my servant, that you have shown
my letter, and betrayed us. Was this well done, young gentleman?

Tony. Here's another. Ask miss there who betrayed you.
Ecod, it was her doing, not mine.

Enter MARLOW.

Marlow. So I have been finely used here among you. Ren-
dered contemptible, driven into ill manners, despised, in-
sulted, laughed at.

Tony. Here's another. We shall have old Bedlam broke
loose presently.

Miss Neville. And there, sir, is the gentleman to whom we
all owe every obligation.

Marlow. What can I say to him, a mere boy, an idiot,
whose ignorance and age are a protection.

Hastings. A poor contemptible booby that would but dis-
grace correction.

Miss Neville. Yet with cunning and malice enough to make
himself merry with all our embarrassments.

Hastings. An insensible cub.

Marlow. Replete with tricks and mischief.

Tony. Baw! damme, but I'll fight you both one after the
other,—with baskets.[29]

Marlow. As for him, he's below resentment. But your conduct, Mr. Hastings, requires an explanation. You knew of my
mistakes, yet would not undeceive me.

Hastings. Tortured as I am with my own disappointments,
is this a time for explanations? It is not friendly, Mr. Marlow.

Marlow. But, sir—

Miss Neville. Mr. Marlow, we never kept on your mistake,
till it was too late to undeceive you. Be pacified.

Enter SERVANT.

Servant. My mistress desires you'll get ready immediately,
madam. The horses are putting to. Your hat and things are in

the next room. We are to go thirty miles before morning.

                                                                Exit.

Miss Neville. Well, well; I'll come presently.

Marlow. (*To* HASTINGS.) Was it well done, sir, to assist in rendering me ridiculous? To hang me out for the scorn of all my acquaintance? Depend upon it, sir, I shall expect an explanation.

Hastings. Was it well done, sir, if you're upon that subject to deliver what I entrusted to yourself to the care of another, sir?

Miss Neville. Mr. Hastings! Mr. Marlow! Why will you increase my distress by this groundless dispute? I implore, I intreat you—

Enter SERVANT.

Servant. Your cloak, madam. My mistress is impatient.

Miss Neville. I come. (*Exit* SERVANT.) Pray be pacified. If I leave you thus, I shall die with apprehension.

Enter SERVANT

Servant. Your fan, muff, and gloves, madam. The horses are waiting.

Miss Neville. Oh, Mr. Marlow! if you knew what a scene of constraint and ill-nature lies before me, I'm sure it would convert your resentment into pity.

Marlow. I'm so distracted with a variety of passions that I don't know what I do. Forgive me, madam. George, forgive me. You know my hasty temper, and should not exasperate it.

Hastings. The torture of my situation is my only excuse.

Miss Neville. Well, my dear Hastings, if you have that esteem for me that I think, that I am sure you have, your constancy for three years will but increase the happiness of our future connection. If—

Mrs. Hardcastle. (*Within.*) Miss Neville! Constance, why Constance, I say!

Miss Neville. I'm coming. Well, constancy. Remember, constancy is the word.   *Exit.*

Hastings. My heart! How can I support this. To be so near happiness, and such happiness.

Marlow. (*To* TONY.) You see now, young gentleman, the effects of your folly. What might be amusement to you, is here disappointment, and even distress.

Tony. (*From a reverie.*) Ecod, I have hit it. It's here. Your hands. Yours and yours, my poor Sulky. My boots there, ho! Meet me two hours hence at the bottom of the garden; and if you don't find Tony Lumpkin a more good-natured fellow than you thought for, I'll give you leave to take my best horse and Bet Bouncer into the bargain. Come along. My boots, ho! *Exeunt.*

ACT V

SCENE I: *The house.*

Enter HASTINGS *and* SERVANT.

Hastings. You saw the old lady and Miss Neville drive off, you say?

Servant. Yes, your honor. They went off in a post coach, and the young 'Squire went on horseback. They're thirty miles off by this time.

Hastings. Then all my hopes are over.

Servant. Yes, sir. Old Sir Charles is arrived. He and the old gentleman of the house have been laughing at Mr. Marlow's mistake this half hour. They are coming this way.

Hastings. Then I must not be seen. So now to my fruitless appointment at the bottom of the garden. This is about the time. *Exit.*

Enter SIR CHARLES *and* HARDCASTLE.

Hardcastle. Ha! ha! ha! The peremptory tone in which he sent forth his sublime commands.

Sir Charles. And the reserve with which I suppose he treated all your advances.

Hardcastle. And yet he might have seen something in me above a common inn-keeper, too.

Sir Charles. Yes, Dick, but he mistook you for an uncommon inn-keeper, ha! ha! ha!

Hardcastle. Well, I'm in too good spirits to think of anything but joy. Yes, my dear friend, this union of our families will make our personal friendships hereditary; and though my daughter's fortune is but small—

Sir Charles. Why, Dick, will you talk of fortune to *me.* My son is possessed of more than a competence already, and can want nothing but a good and virtuous girl to share his happiness and increase it. If they like each other as you say they do—

Hardcastle. If, man! I tell you they *do* like each other. My daughter as good as told me so.

Sir Charles. But girls are apt to flatter themselves, you know.

Hardcastle. I saw him grasp her hand in the warmest manner myself; and here he comes to put you out of your *ifs*, I warrant him.

Enter MARLOW.

Marlow. I come, sir, once more, to ask your pardon for my strange conduct. I can scarce reflect on my insolence without confusion.

Hardcastle. Tut, boy, a trifle. You take it too gravely. An hour or two's laughing with my daughter will set all to rights again. She'll never like you the worse for it.

Marlow. Sir, I shall be always proud of her approbation.

Hardcastle. Approbation is but a cold word, Mr. Marlow; if I am not deceived, you have something more than approbation thereabouts. You take me.

Marlow. Really, sir, I have not that happiness.

Hardcastle. Come, boy, I'm an old fellow, and know what's what, as well as you that are younger. I know what has past between you; but mum.

Marlow. Sure, sir, nothing has past between us but the most profound respect on my side, and the most distant reserve on hers. You don't think, sir, that my impudence has been past upon all the rest of the family?

Hardcastle. Impudence! No, I don't say that—Not quite impudence—Though girls like to be played with, and rumpled a little, too, sometimes. But she has told no tales, I assure you.

Marlow. I never gave her the slightest cause.

Hardcastle. Well, well, I like modesty in its place well enough. But this is over-acting, young gentleman. You may be open. Your father and I will like you the better for it.

Marlow. May I die, sir, if I ever—

Hardcastle. I tell you, she don't dislike you; and as I'm sure you like her—

Marlow. Dear sir—I protest, sir,—

Hardcastle. I see no reason why you should not be joined as fast as the parson can tie you.

Marlow. But hear me, sir—

Hardcastle. Your father approves the match, I admire it, every moment's delay will be doing mischief, so—

Marlow. But why won't you hear me? By all that's just and true, I never gave Miss Hardcastle the slightest mark of my attachment, or even the most distant hint to suspect me of a affection. We had but one interview, and that was formal, modest and uninteresting.

Hardcastle. (*Aside.*) This fellow's formal, modest impudence is beyond bearing.

Sir Charles. And you never grasped her hand, or made any protestations!

Marlow. As heaven is my witness, I came down in obedience to your commands. I saw the lady without emotion, and parted without reluctance. I hope you'll exact no further proofs of my duty, nor prevent me from leaving a house in which I suffer so many mortifications.   *Exit.*

Sir Charles. I'm astonished at the air of sincerity with which he parted.

Hardcastle. And I'm astonished at the deliberate intrepidity of his assurance.

Sir Charles. I pledge my life and honor upon his truth.

Hardcastle. Here comes my daughter, and I would stake my happiness upon her veracity.

Enter Miss Hardcastle.

Hardcastle. Kate, come hither, child. Answer us sincerely, and without reserve; has Mr. Marlow made you any professions of love and affection?

Miss Hardcastle. The question is very abrupt, sir! But since you require unreserved sincerity, I think he has.

Hardcastle. (*To* Sir Charles.) You see.

Sir Charles. And pray, madam, have you and my son had more than one interview?

Miss Hardcastle. Yes, sir, several.

Hardcastle. (*To* Sir Charles.) You see.

Sir Charles. But did he profess any attachment?

Miss Hardcastle. A lasting one.

Sir Charles. Did he talk of love?

Miss Hardcastle. Much, sir.

Sir Charles. Amazing! And all this formally?

Miss Hardcastle. Formally.

Hardcastle. Now, my friend, I hope you are satisfied.

Sir Charles. And how did he behave, Madam?

Miss Hardcastle. As most professed admirers do. Said some civil things of my face, talked much of his want of merit, and the greatness of mine; mentioned his heart, and gave a short tragedy speech, and ended with pretended rapture.

Sir Charles. Now I'm perfectly convinced, indeed. I know his conversation among women to be modest and submissive. This forward, canting, ranting manner by no means describes him, and I am confident, he never sat for the picture.

Miss Hardcastle. Then what, sir, if I should convince you to your face of my sincerity? If you and my papa, in about half an hour, will place yourselves behind that screen, you shall hear him declare his passion to me in person.

Sir Charles. Agreed. And if I find him what you describe, all my happiness in him must have an end.   *Exit.*

Miss Hardcastle. And if you don't find him what I describe —I fear my happiness must never have a beginning. *Exeunt.*

SCENE II: *Scene changes to the back of the garden.*

Enter HASTINGS.

Hastings. What an idiot am I, to wait here for a fellow, who probably takes delight in mortifying me. He never intended to be punctual, and I'll wait no longer. What do I see! It is he, and perhaps with news of my Constance.

Enter TONY, *booted and spattered.*

Hastings. My honest squire! I now find you a man of your word. This looks like friendship.

Tony. Ay, I'm your friend, and the best friend you have in the world, if you knew but all. This riding by night, by the bye, is cursedly tiresome. It has shook me worse than the basket of a stage-coach.

Hastings. But how? Where did you leave your fellow travellers? Are they in safety? Are they housed?

Tony. Five and twenty miles in two hours and a half is no such bad driving. The poor beasts have smoked for it: Rabbit me, but I'd rather ride forty miles after a fox, than ten with such *varment.*

Hastings. Well, but where have you left the ladies? I die with impatience.

Tony. Left them? Why, where should I leave them, but where I found them?

Hastings. This is a riddle.

Tony. Riddle me this then. What's that goes round the house, and round the house, and never touches the house?

Hastings. I'm still astray.

Tony. Why that's it, mon. I have led them astray. By jingo, there's not a pond or slough within five miles of the place but they can tell the taste of.

Hastings. Ha, ha, ha, I understand; you took them in a

round, while they supposed themselves going forward. And so you have at last brought them home again.

Tony. You shall hear. I first took them down Feather-bed-lane, where we stuck fast in the mud. I then rattled them crack over the stones of Up-and-down Hill—I then introduced them to the gibbet on Heavy-tree Heath, and from that, with a circumbendibus, I fairly lodged them in the horse-pond at the bottom of the garden.

Hastings. But no accident, I hope.

Tony. No, no! Only mother is confoundedly frightened. She thinks herself forty miles off. She's sick of the journey, and the cattle can scarce crawl. So if your own horses be ready, you may whip off with cousin, and I'll be bound that no soul here can budge a foot to follow you.

Hastings. My dear friend, how can I be grateful?

Tony. Ay, now it's "dear friend," "noble squire." Just now, it was all "idiot," "cub," and "run me through the guts." Damn *your* way of fighting, I say. After we take a knock in this part of the country, we kiss and be friends. But if you had run me through the guts, then I should be dead, and you might go kiss the hangman.

Hastings. The rebuke is just. But I must hasten to relieve Miss Neville; if you keep the old lady employed, I promise to take care of the young one.   *Exit.*

Tony. Never fear me. Here she comes. Vanish. She's got from the pond, and draggled up to the waist like a mermaid.

Enter MRS. HARDCASTLE.

Mrs. Hardcastle. Oh, Tony, I'm killed! Shook! Battered to death! I shall never survive it. That last jolt that laid us against the quickset hedge has done my business.

Tony. Alack, mama, it was all your own fault. You would be for running away by night, without knowing one inch of the way.

Mrs. Hardcastle. I wish we were at home again. I never met so many accidents in so short a journey. Drenched in the mud, overturned in a ditch, stuck fast in a slough, jolted to a jelly, and at last to lose our way. Whereabouts do you think we are, Tony?

Tony. By my guess we should be upon Crackskull common, about forty miles from home.

Mrs. Hardcastle. O lud! O lud! the most notorious spot in all the country. We only want a robbery to make a complete night on't.

Tony. Don't be afraid, mama, don't be afraid. Two of the five that kept here are hanged, and the other three may not

find us. Don't be afraid. Is that a man that's galloping behind us? No; it's only a tree. Don't be afraid.

Mrs. Hardcastle. The fright will certainly kill me.

Tony. Do you see anything like a black hat moving behind
the thicket?

Mrs. Hardcastle. O death!

Tony. No, it's only a cow. Don't be afraid, mama; don't
be afraid!

Mrs. Hardcastle. As I'm alive, Tony, I see a man coming
towards us. Ah! I'm sure on't. If he perceives us, we are undone.

Tony. (*Aside.*) Father-in-law, by all that's unlucky, come
to take one of his night walks. (*To her.*) Ah, it's a highwayman, with pistols as long as my arm. A damned ill-looking
fellow.

Mrs. Hardcastle. Good heaven defend us! He approaches!

Tony. Do you hide yourself in that thicket, and leave me
to manage him. If there be danger, I'll cough, and cry hem.
When I cough be sure to keep close.

(MRS. HARDCASTLE *hides behind a tree in the back scene.*)

Enter HARDCASTLE.

Hardcastle. I'm mistaken, or I heard voices of people in
want of help. Oh, Tony, is that you? I did not expect you
so soon back. Are your mother and her charge in safety?

Tony. Very safe, sir, at my Aunt Pedigree's. Hem.

Mrs. Hardcastle. (*From behind.*) Ah death! I find there's
danger.

Hardcastle. Forty miles in three hours; sure, that's too
much, my youngster.

Tony. Stout horses and willing minds make short journies,
as they say. Hem.

Mrs. Hardcastle. (*From behind.*) Sure he'll do the dear boy
no harm.

Hardcastle. But I heard a voice here; I should be glad to
know from whence it came?

Tony. It was I, sir, talking to myself, sir. I was saying that
forty miles in four hours was very good going. Hem! As to
be sure it was. Hem! I have got a sort of cold by being out
in the air. We'll go in, if you please. Hem!

Hardcastle. But if you talk'd to yourself, you did not answer yourself. I am certain I heard two voices, and am resolved (*raising his voice*) to find the other out.

Mrs. Hardcastle. (*From behind.*) Oh! he's coming to find
me out. Oh!

Tony. What need you go, sir, if I tell you? Hem. I'll lay down my life for the truth—hem—I'll tell you all, sir.

               (*Detaining him.*)

Hardcastle. I tell you, I will not be detained. I insist on seeing. It's in vain to expect I'll believe you.

Mrs. Hardcastle. (*Running forward from behind.*) O lud, he'll murder my poor boy, my darling. Here, good gentleman, whet your rage upon me. Take my money, my life, but spare that young gentleman, spare my child, if you have any mercy!

Hardcastle. My wife! as I'm a Christian. From whence can she come, or what does she mean?

Mrs. Hardcastle. (*Kneeling.*) Take compassion on us, good Mr. Highwayman. Take our money, our watches, all we have, but spare our lives. We will never bring you to justice, indeed we won't, good Mr. Highwayman.

Hardcastle. I believe the woman's out of her senses. What, Dorothy, don't you know *me?*

Mrs. Hardcastle. Mr. Hardcastle, as I'm alive! My fears blinded me. But who, my dear, could have expected to meet you here, in this frightful place, so far from home? What has brought you to follow us?

Hardcastle. Sure, Dorothy, you have not lost your wits. So far from home, when you are within forty yards of your own door. (*To him.*) This is one of your old tricks, you graceless rogue you. (*To her.*) Don't you know the gate, and the mulberry-tree; and don't you remember the horse-pond, my dear?

Mrs. Hardcastle. Yes, I shall remember the horse-pond as long as I live; I have caught my death in it. (*To* TONY.) And is it to you, you graceless varlet, I owe all this? I'll teach you to abuse your mother, I will.

Tony. Ecod, mother, all the parish says you have spoiled me, and so you may take the fruits on't.

Mrs. Hardcastle. I'll spoil you, I will.

           Follows him off stage. Exeunt.

Hardcastle. There's morality, however, in his reply.   *Exit.*

Enter HASTINGS *and* MISS NEVILLE.

Hastings. My dear Constance, why will you deliberate thus? If we delay a moment, all is lost for ever. Pluck up a little resolution, and we shall soon be out of reach of her malignity.

Miss Neville. I find it impossible. My spirits are so sunk with the agitations I have suffered, that I am unable to face any new danger. Two or three years patience will at last crown us with happiness.

Hastings. Such a tedious delay is worse than inconstancy. Let us fly, my charmer. Let us date our happiness from this very moment. Perish fortune. Love and content will increase what we possess beyond a monarch's revenue. Let me prevail.

Miss Neville. No, Mr. Hastings; no. Prudence once more comes to my relief, and I will obey its dictates. In the moment of passion, fortune may be despised, but it produces a lasting repentance. I'm resolved to apply to Mr. Hardcastle's compassion and justice for redress.

Hastings. But though he has the will, he has not the power to relieve you.

Miss Neville. But he has influence, and upon that I am resolved to rely.

Hastings. I have no hopes. But since you persist, I must reluctantly obey you.   *Exeunt.*

SCENE III: *Scene changes to the parlor.*

Enter SIR CHARLES *and* MISS HARDCASTLE.

Sir Charles. What a situation am I in. If what you say appears, I shall then find a guilty son. If what he says be true, I shall then lose one that, of all others, I most wished for a daughter.

Miss Hardcastle. I am proud of your approbation, and to show I merit it, if you place yourselves as I directed, you shall hear his explicit declaration. But he comes.

Sir Charles. I'll to your father, and keep him to the appointment.   *Exit.*

Enter MARLOW.

Marlow. Though prepared for setting out, I come once more to take leave, nor did I, till this moment, know the pain I feel in the separation.

Miss Hardcastle. (*In her own natural manner.*) I believe these sufferings cannot be very great, sir, which you can so easily remove. A day or two longer, perhaps, might lessen your uneasiness, by showing the little value of what you now think proper to regret.

Marlow. (*Aside.*) This girl every moment improves upon me. (*To her.*) It must not be, madam. I have already trifled too long with my heart. My very pride begins to submit to my passion. The disparity of education and fortune, the anger of a parent, and the contempt of my equals, begin to lose their weight; and nothing can restore me to myself but this painful effort of resolution.

Miss Hardcastle. Then go, sir. I'll urge nothing more to detain you. Though my family be as good as hers you came down to visit, and my education, I hope, not inferior, what are these advantages without equal affluence? I must remain contented with the slight approbation of imputed merit; I must have only the mockery of your addresses, while all your serious aims are fixed on fortune.

Enter HARDCASTLE *and* SIR CHARLES *from behind.*

Sir Charles. Here, behind this screen.

Hardcastle. Ay, ay, make no noise. I'll engage my Kate covers him with confusion at last.

Marlow. By heavens, madam, fortune was ever my smallest consideration. Your beauty at first caught my eye; for who could see that without emotion? But every moment that I converse with you steals in some new grace, heightens the picture and gives it stronger expression. What at first seemed rustic plainness, now appears refined simplicity. What seemed forward assurance, now strikes me as the result of courageous innocence, and conscious virtue.

Sir Charles. What can it mean! He amazes me!

Hardcastle. I told you how it would be. Hush!

Marlow. I am now determined to stay, madam, and I have too good an opinion of my father's discernment, when he sees you, to doubt his approbation.

Miss Hardcastle. No, Mr. Marlow, I will not, cannot detain you. Do you think I could suffer a connection, in which there is the smallest room for repentance? Do you think I would take the mean advantage of a transient passion, to load you with confusion? Do you think I could ever relish that happiness, which was acquired by lessening yours?

Marlow. By all that's good, I can have no happiness but what's in your power to grant me. Nor shall I ever feel repentance, but in not having seen your merits before. I will stay, even contrary to your wishes; and though you should persist to shun me, I will make my respectful assiduities atone for the levity of my past conduct.

Miss Hardcastle. Sir, I must entreat you'll desist. As our acquaintance began, so let it end, in indifference. I might have given an hour or two to levity; but seriously, Mr. Marlow, do you think I could ever submit to a connection, where *I* must appear mercenary, and *you* imprudent? Do you think I could ever catch at the confident addresses of a secure admirer?

Marlow. (*Kneeling*.) Does this look like security? Does this look like confidence? No, madam, every moment that shows me your merit, only serves to increase my diffidence and confusion. Here let me continue—

Sir Charles. I can hold it no longer! Charles, Charles, how hast thou deceived me! Is this your indifference, your uninteresting conversation?

Hardcastle. Your cold contempt; your formal interview! What have you to say now?

Marlow. That I'm all amazement. What can it mean!

Hardcastle. It means that you can say and unsay things at pleasure. That you can address a lady in private, and deny it in public; that you have one story for us, and another for my daughter.

Marlow. Daughter!—this lady your daughter!

Hardcastle. Yes, sir, my only daughter. My Kate, whose else should she be?

Marlow. Oh, the devil!

Miss Hardcastle. Yes, sir, that very identical tall, squinting lady you were pleased to take me for. (*Curtsying*.) She that you addressed as the mild, modest, sentimental man of gravity, and the bold, forward, agreeable Rattle of the Ladies Club; ha, ha, ha.

Marlow. Zounds, there's no bearing this; it's worse than death.

Miss Hardcastle. In which of your characters, Sir, will you give us leave to address you? As the faltering gentleman, with looks on the ground, that speaks just to be heard, and hates hypocrisy; or the loud, confident creature, that keeps it up with Mrs. Mantrap, and old Miss Biddy Buckskin, till three in the morning; ha, ha, ha!

Marlow. Oh, curse on my noisy head. I never attempted to be impudent yet, that I was not taken down. I must be gone.

Hardcastle. By the hand of my body, but you shall not. I see it was all a mistake, and I am rejoiced to find it. You shall not, sir, I tell you. I know she'll forgive you. Won't you forgive him, Kate? We'll all forgive you. Take courage, man.

They retire, she tormenting him, to the back scene.

Enter MRS. HARDCASTLE, TONY.

Mrs. Hardcastle. So, so they're gone off. Let them go, I care not.

Hardcastle. Who gone?

Mrs. Hardcastle. My dutiful niece and her gentleman, Mr. Hastings, from town. He who came down with our modest visitor here.

Sir Charles. Who, my honest George Hastings? As worthy a fellow as lives, and the girl could not have made a more prudent choice.

Hardcastle. Then, by the hand of my body, I'm proud of the connection.

Mrs. Hardcastle. Well, if he has taken away the lady, he has not taken her fortune; that remains in this family to console us for her loss.

Hardcastle. Sure, Dorothy, you would not be so mercenary?

Mrs. Hardcastle. Ay, that's my affair, not yours.

Hardcastle.[30] But you know if your son, when of age, refuses to marry his cousin, her whole fortune is then at her own disposal.

Mrs. Hardcastle. Ay, but he's not of age, and she has not thought proper to wait for his refusal.

Enter Hastings *and* Miss Neville.

Mrs. Hardcastle. (*Aside.*) What! returned so soon? I begin not to like it.

Hastings. (*To* Hardcastle.) For my late attempt to fly off with your niece, let my present confusion be my punishment. We are now come back, to appeal from your justice to your humanity. By her father's consent, I first paid her my addresses, and our passions were first founded in duty.

Miss Neville. Since his death, I have been obliged to stoop to dissimulation to avoid oppression. In an hour of levity, I was ready even to give up my fortune to secure my choice. But I'm now recovered from the delusion, and hope from your tenderness what is denied me from a nearer connection.

Mrs. Hardcastle. Pshaw, pshaw, this is all but the whining end of a modern novel.

Hardcastle. Be it what it will, I'm glad they're come back to reclaim their due. Come hither, Tony boy. Do you refuse this lady's hand whom I now offer you?

Tony. What signifies my refusing? You know I can't refuse her till I'm of age, father.

Hardcastle. While I thought concealing your age, boy, was likely to conduce to your improvement, I concurred with your mother's desire to keep it secret. But since I find she turns it to a wrong use, I must now declare, you have been of age these three months.

Tony. Of age! Am I of age, father?

Hardcastle. Above three months.

Tony. Then you'll see the first use I'll make of my liberty. (*Taking* Miss Neville's *hand.*) Witness all men by these present, that I, Anthony Lumpkin, Esquire, of Blank place, refuse you, Constantia Neville, spinster, of no place at all, for my true and lawful wife. So Constance Neville may marry whom she pleases, and Tony Lumpkin is his own man again!

Sir Charles. O brave squire!

Hastings. My worthy friend!

Mrs. Hardcastle. My undutiful offspring!

Marlow. Joy, my dear George, I give you joy sincerely. And could I prevail upon my little tyrant here to be less arbitrary, I should be the happiest man alive, if you would return me the favor.

Hastings. (*To* Miss Hardcastle.) Come, madam, you are now driven to the very last scene of all your contrivances. I know you like him, I'm sure he loves you, and you must and shall have him.

Hardcastle. (*Joining their hands.*) And I say so too. And Mr. Marlow, if she makes as good a wife as she has a daughter, I don't believe you'll ever repent your bargain. So now to supper; tomorrow we shall gather all the poor of the parish about us, and the Mistakes of the Night shall be crowned with a merry morning; so boy, take her; and as you have been mistaken in the mistress, my wish is, that you may never be mistaken in the wife.

EPILOGUE

By Dr. Goldsmith

Spoken by Miss Hardcastle.

Well, having stooped to conquer with success,
And gained a husband without aid from dress,
Still as a Barmaid, I could wish it too,
As I have conquered him to conquer you:
And let me say, for all your resolution,
That pretty Barmaids have done execution.
Our life is all a play, composed to please,
"We have our exits and our entrances."
The first act shows the simple country maid,
Harmless and young, of everything afraid;
Blushes when hired, and with unmeaning action,
'I hopes as how to give you satisfaction.'
Her second act displays a livelier scene,—
The unblushing Barmaid of a country inn,
Who whisks about the house, at market caters,
Talks loud, coquets the guests, and scolds the waiters.
Next the scene shifts to town, and there she soars,
The chop-house toast of ogling connoisseurs.
On 'squires and cits she there displays her arts,
And on the gridiron broils her lovers' hearts—
And as she smiles, her triumphs to complete,
Even Common Councilmen forget to eat.
The fourth act shows her wedded to the 'Squire,
And madam now begins to hold it higher;
Pretends to taste, at Operas cries 'Caro,'
And quits her Nancy Dawson,[31] for *'Che Faro.'*[32]
Doats upon dancing, and in all her pride,
Swims round the room, the Heinel [33] of Cheapside:
Ogles and leers with artificial skill,
Till having lost in age the power to kill,
She sits all night at cards, and ogles at spadille.[34]
Such, through our lives, the eventful history—
The fifth and last act still remains for me.
The Barmaid now for your protection prays,
Turns female barrister, and pleads for Bayes.[35]

EPILOGUE

By J. Craddock, Esq.

Spoken by Tony Lumpkin.

Well—now all's ended—and my comrades gone,
Pray what becomes of mother's only son?
A hopeful blade!—in town I'll fix my station,
And try to make a bluster in the nation.
As for my cousin Neville, I renounce her,
Off—in a crack—I'll carry big Bett Bouncer.
Why should not I in the great world appear?
I soon shall have a thousand pounds a year;
No matter what a man may here inherit,
In London—'gad, they've some regard to spirit.
I see the horses prancing up the streets,
And big Bett Bouncer bobs to all she meets;
Then hoikes to jiggs and pastimes every night—
Not to the plays—they say it a'n't polite,
To Sadler's Wells perhaps, or operas go,
And once, by chance, to the roratorio.
Thus here and there, for ever up and down,
We'll set the fashions, too, to half the town;
And then at auctions—money ne'er regard,
Buy pictures like the great, ten pounds a yard;
Zounds, we shall make these London gentry say,
We know what's damn'd genteel, as well as they.

The School for Scandal

by
Richard Brinsley Sheridan

PROLOGUE

By Mr. Garrick

Spoken by Sir Peter Teazle.

A School for Scandal! tell me, I beseech you,
Needs there a school this modish art to teach you?
No need of lessons now, the knowing think;
We might as well be taught to eat and drink.
Caused by a dearth of scandal, should the vapors
Distress our fair ones—let them read the papers;
Their powerful mixtures such disorders hit;
Crave what you will—there's *quantum sufficit.*[1]
"Lord!" cries my Lady Wormwood (who loves tattle,
And puts much salt and pepper in her prattle),
Just risen at noon, all night at cards when threshing
Strong tea and scandal—"Bless me, how refreshing!
Give me the papers, Lisp—how bold and free!   (*Sips.*)
Last night Lord L.—(*Sips.*) *was caught with Lady D.*
For aching heads what charming sal volatile!   (*Sips.*)
If Mrs. B. will still continue flirting,
We hope she'll DRAW, *or we'll* UNDRAW *the curtain.*
Fine satire, poz[2]—in public all abuse it,
But, by ourselves—(*Sips.*) our praise we can't refuse it.
Now, Lisp, read you—there at that dash and star."
"Yes, ma'am—*A certain Lord had best beware,*
Who lives not twenty miles from Grosvenor Square;
For should he Lady W. find willing,
Wormwood is bitter"——"Oh! that's me! the villain!
Throw it behind the fire, and never more
Let that vile paper come within my door."
Thus at our friends we laugh, who feel the dart;
To reach our feelings, we ourselves must smart.
Is our young bard so young, to think that he
Can stop the full spring-tide of calumny?

67

Knows he the world so little, and its trade?
Alas! the devil's sooner raised than laid.
So strong, so swift, the monster there's no gagging:
Cut Scandal's head off, still the tongue is wagging.
Proud of your smiles once lavishly bestowed,
Again our young Don Quixote takes the road;
To show his gratitude he draws his pen,
And seeks his hydra, Scandal, in his den.
For your applause all perils he would through—
He'll fight—that's *write*—a cavalliero true,
Till every drop of blood—that's *ink*—is spilt for you.

DRAMATIS PERSONÆ

SIR PETER TEAZLE
SIR OLIVER SURFACE
JOSEPH SURFACE
CHARLES SURFACE
CARELESS
SNAKE
SIR BENJAMIN BACKBITE
CRABTREE
ROWLEY
MOSES
TRIP
SIR TOBY BUMPER [3]

LADY TEAZLE
MARIA
LADY SNEERWELL
MRS. CANDOUR

Gentlemen, Maid, *and* Servants.

Scene—LONDON.

ACT I

Scene I: Lady Sneerwell's *Dressing-room.*

Lady Sneerwell *at her toilet;* Snake *drinking chocolate.*

Lady Sneerwell. The paragraphs, you say, Mr. Snake, were all inserted?

Snake. They were, madam; and, as I copied them myself in a feigned hand, there can be no suspicion whence they came.

Lady Sneerwell. Did you circulate the report of Lady Brittle's intrigue with Captain Boastall?

Snake. That's in as fine a train as your ladyship could wish. In the common course of things, I think it must reach Mrs. Clackitt's ears within four-and-twenty hours; and then, you know, the business is as good as done.

Lady Sneerwell. Why, truly, Mrs. Clackitt has a very pretty talent, and a great deal of industry.

Snake. True, madam, and has been tolerably successful in her day. To my knowledge, she has been the cause of six matches being broken off, and three sons being disinherited; of four forced elopements, and as many close confinements; nine separate maintenances, and two divorces. Nay, I have more than once traced her causing a *tête-à-tête* in the *Town and Country Magazine,*[4] when the parties, perhaps, had never seen each other's face before in the course of their lives.

Lady Sneerwell. She certainly has talents, but her manner is gross.

Snake. 'Tis very true. She generally designs well, has a free tongue and a bold invention; but her coloring is too dark, and her outlines often extravagant. She wants that delicacy of tint, and mellowness of sneer, which distinguish your ladyship's scandal.

Lady Sneerwell. You are partial, Snake.

Snake. Not in the least; everybody allows that Lady Sneerwell can do more with a word or look than many can with the most labored detail, even when they happen to have a little truth on their side to support it.

Lady Sneerwell. Yes, my dear Snake; and I am no hypocrite to deny the satisfaction I reap from the success of my efforts. Wounded myself in the early part of my life, by the envenomed tongue of slander, I confess I have since known no pleasure equal to the reducing others to the level of my own injured reputation.

Snake. Nothing can be more natural. But, Lady Sneerwell, there is one affair in which you have lately employed me, wherein, I confess, I am at a loss to guess your motives.

Lady Sneerwell. I conceive you mean with respect to my neighbor, Sir Peter Teazle, and his family?

Snake. I do. Here are two young men, to whom Sir Peter has acted as a kind of guardian since their father's death; the eldest possessing the most amiable character, and universally well spoken of—the youngest, the most dissipated and extravagant young fellow in the kingdom, without friends or character: the former an avowed admirer of your ladyship, and apparently your favorite; the latter attached to Maria, Sir Peter's ward, and confessedly beloved by her. Now, on the face of these circumstances, it is utterly unaccountable to me why you, the widow of a city knight,⁵ with a good jointure, should not close with the passion of a man of such character and expectations as Mr. Surface; and more so, why you should be so uncommonly earnest to destroy the mutual attachment subsisting between his brother Charles and Maria.

Lady Sneerwell. Then, at once to unravel this mystery, I must inform you that love has no share whatever in the intercourse between Mr. Surface and me.

Snake. No!

Lady Sneerwell. His real attachment is to Maria or her fortune; but, finding in his brother a favorite rival, he has been obliged to mask his pretensions and profit by my assistance.

Snake. Yet still I am more puzzled why you should interest yourself in his success.

Lady Sneerwell. Heavens! how dull you are! Cannot you surmise the weakness which I hitherto, through shame, have concealed even from you? Must I confess that Charles—that libertine, that extravagant, that bankrupt in fortune and reputation—that he it is for whom I am thus anxious and malicious, and to gain whom I would sacrifice everything?

Snake. Now, indeed, your conduct appears consistent; but how came you and Mr. Surface so confidential?

Lady Sneerwell. For our mutual interest. I have found him out a long time since. I know him to be artful, selfish, and malicious—in short, a sentimental knave; while with Sir Peter, and indeed with all his acquaintance, he passes for a youthful miracle of prudence, good sense, and benevolence.

Snake. Yes! yet Sir Peter vows he has not his equal in England; and, above all, he praises him as a man of sentiment.

Lady Sneerwell. True; and with the assistance of his sentiment and hypocrisy he has brought Sir Peter entirely into his interest with regard to Maria; while poor Charles has no friend in the house—though, I fear, he has a powerful one in Maria's heart, against whom we must direct our schemes.

Enter SERVANT.

Servant. Mr. Surface.

Lady Sneerwell. Show him up. (*Exit* SERVANT.) He generally calls about this time. I don't wonder at people giving him to me for a lover.

Enter JOSEPH SURFACE.

Joseph Surface. My dear Lady Sneerwell, how do you do today? Mr. Snake, your most obedient.

Lady Sneerwell. Snake has just been rallying me on our mutual attachment; but I have informed him of our real views. You know how useful he has been to us; and, believe me, the confidence is not ill placed.

Joseph Surface. Madam, it is impossible for me to suspect a man of Mr. Snake's sensibility and discernment.

Lady Sneerwell. Well, well, no compliments now; but tell me when you saw your mistress, Maria—or, what is more material to me, your brother.

Joseph Surface. I have not seen either since I left you; but I can inform you that they never meet. Some of your stories have taken a good effect on Maria.

Lady Sneerwell. Ah, my dear Snake! the merit of this belongs to you. But do your brother's distresses increase?

Joseph Surface. Every hour. I am told he has had another execution in the house yesterday. In short, his dissipation and extravagance exceed anything I have ever heard of.

Lady Sneerwell. Poor Charles!

Joseph Surface. True, madam; notwithstanding his vices, one can't help feeling for him. Poor Charles! I'm sure I wish it were in my power to be of any essential service to him; for the man who does not share in the distresses of a brother, even though merited by his own misconduct, deserves——

Lady Sneerwell. O Lud! you are going to be moral and forget that you are among friends.

Joseph Surface. Egad, that's true! I'll keep that sentiment till I see Sir Peter. However, it is certainly a charity to rescue Maria from such a libertine, who, if he is to be reclaimed, can be so only by a person of your ladyship's superior accomplishments and understanding.

Snake. I believe, Lady Sneerwell, here's company coming.

I'll go and copy the letter I mentioned to you. Mr. Surface, your most obedient.

Joseph Surface. Sir, your very devoted. (*Exit* SNAKE.) Lady Sneerwell, I am very sorry you have put any further confidence in that fellow.

Lady Sneerwell. Why so?

Joseph Surface. I have lately detected him in frequent conference with old Rowley, who was formerly my father's steward and has never, you know, been a friend of mine.

Lady Sneerwell. And do you think he would betray us?

Joseph Surface. Nothing more likely: take my word for't, Lady Sneerwell, that fellow hasn't virtue enough to be faithful even to his own villainy. Ah, Maria!

Enter MARIA.

Lady Sneerwell. Maria, my dear, how do you do? What's the matter?

Maria. Oh! there's that disagreeable lover of mine, Sir Benjamin Backbite, has just called at my guardian's with his odious uncle, Crabtree; so I slipped out and ran hither to avoid them.

Lady Sneerwell. Is that all?

Joseph Surface. If my brother Charles had been of the party, madam, perhaps you would not have been so much alarmed.

Lady Sneerwell. Nay, now you are severe; for I dare swear the truth of the matter is, Maria heard you were here. But, my dear, what has Sir Benjamin done that you should avoid him so?

Maria. Oh, he has done nothing—but 'tis for what he has said. His conversation is a perpetual libel on all his acquaintance.

Joseph Surface. Ay, and the worst of it is, there is no advantage in not knowing him, for he'll abuse a stranger just as soon as his best friend; and his uncle's as bad.

Lady Sneerwell. Nay, but we should make allowance; Sir Benjamin is a wit and a poet.

Maria. For my part, I own, madam, wit loses its respect with me when I see it in company with malice. What do you think, Mr. Surface?

Joseph Surface. Certainly, madam. To smile at the jest which plants a thorn in another's breast is to become a principal in the mischief.

Lady Sneerwell. Psha! there's no possibility of being witty without a little ill nature. The malice of a good thing is the barb that makes it stick. What's your opinion, Mr. Surface?

Joseph Surface. To be sure, madam; that conversation, where the spirit of raillery is suppressed, will ever appear tedious and insipid.

Maria. Well, I'll not debate how far scandal may be allowable; but in a man, I am sure, it is always contemptible. We have pride, envy, rivalship, and a thousand motives to depreciate each other; but the male slanderer must have the cowardice of a woman before he can traduce one.

Enter SERVANT.

Servant. Madam, Mrs. Candour is below, and, if your ladyship's at leisure, will leave her carriage.

Lady Sneerwell. Beg her to walk in. (*Exit* SERVANT.) Now, Maria, here is a character to your taste; for, though Mrs. Candour is a little talkative, everybody knows her to be the best natured and best sort of woman.

Maria. Yes, with a very gross affection of good nature and benevolence, she does more mischief than the direct malice of old Crabtree.

Joseph Surface. I'faith that's true, Lady Sneerwell: whenever I hear the current running against the characters of my friends, I never think them in such danger as when Candour undertakes their defence.

Lady Sneerwell. Hush!—here she is!

Enter MRS. CANDOUR.

Mrs. Candour. My dear Lady Sneerwell, how have you been this century?—Mr. Surface, what news do you hear?—though indeed it is no matter, for I think one hears nothing else but scandal.

Joseph Surface. Just so, indeed, ma'am.

Mrs. Candour. Oh, Maria! child—what, is the whole affair off between you and Charles? His extravagance, I presume —the town talks of nothing else.

Maria. I am very sorry, ma'am, the town has so little to do.

Mrs. Candour. True, true, child: but there's no stopping people's tongues. I own I was hurt to hear it, as I indeed was to learn, from the same quarter, that your guardian, Sir Peter, and Lady Teazle have not agreed lately as well as could be wished.

Maria. 'Tis strangely impertinent for people to busy themselves so.

Mrs. Candour. Very true, child; but what's to be done? People will talk—there's no preventing it. Why, it was but yesterday I was told that Miss Gadabout had eloped with

Sir Filagree Flirt. But, Lord! there's no minding what one hears; though, to be sure, I had this from very good authority.

Maria. Such reports are highly scandalous.

Mrs. Candour. So they are, child—shameful, shameful! But the world is so censorious, no character escapes. Lord, now who would have suspected your friend, Miss Prim, of an indiscretion? Yet such is the ill nature of people that they say her uncle stopped her last week just as she was stepping into the York diligence [6] with her dancing-master.

Maria. I'll answer for't there are no grounds for that report.

Mrs. Candour. Ah, no foundation in the world, I dare swear: no more, probably, than for the story circulated last month, of Mrs. Festino's affair with Colonel Cassino—though, to be sure, that matter was never rightly cleared up.

Joseph Surface. The license of invention some people take is monstrous indeed.

Maria. 'Tis so; but, in my opinion, those who report such things are equally culpable.

Mrs. Candour. To be sure they are; tale bearers are as bad as the tale makers—'tis an old observation and a very true one: but what's to be done, as I said before? how will you prevent people from talking? Today, Mrs. Clackitt assured me Mr. and Mrs. Honeymoon were at last become mere man and wife like the rest of their acquaintance. She likewise hinted that a certain widow in the next street had got rid of her dropsy and recovered her shape in a most surprising manner. And at the same time Miss Tattle, who was by, affirmed that Lord Buffalo had discovered his lady at a house of no extraordinary fame; and that Sir Harry Bouquet and Tom Saunter were to measure swords on a similar provocation. But, Lord, do you think I would report these things! No, no! tale bearers, as I said before, are just as bad as the tale makers.

Joseph Surface. Ah! Mrs. Candour, if everybody had your forbearance and good nature!

Mrs. Candour. I confess, Mr. Surface, I cannot bear to hear people attacked behind their backs; and when ugly circumstances come out against our acquaintance, I own I always love to think the best. By-the-bye, I hope 'tis not true that your brother is absolutely ruined?

Joseph Surface. I am afraid his circumstances are very bad indeed, ma'am.

Mrs. Candour. Ah!—I heard so—but you must tell him to keep up his spirits; everybody almost is in the same way:

Lord Spindle, Sir Thomas Splint, Captain Quinze, and Mr. Nickit—all up, I hear, within this week; so, if Charles is undone, he'll find half his acquaintance ruined too; and that, you know, is a consolation.

Joseph Surface. Doubtless, ma'am—a very great one.

Enter SERVANT.

Servant. Mr. Crabtree and Sir Benjamin Backbite.   (*Exit.*)

Lady Sneerwell. So, Maria, you see your lover pursues you; positively you shan't escape.

Enter CRABTREE *and* SIR BENJAMIN BACKBITE.

Crabtree. Lady Sneerwell, I kiss your hand. Mrs. Candour, I don't believe you are acquainted with my nephew, Sir Benjamin Backbite? Egad, ma'am, he has a pretty wit and is a pretty poet too. Isn't he, Lady Sneerwell?

Sir Benjamin. Oh, fie, uncle!

Crabtree. Nay, egad it's true: I back him at a rebus or a charade against the best rhymer in the kingdom. Has your ladyship heard the epigram he wrote last week on Lady Frizzle's feather catching fire?—Do, Benjamin, repeat it, or the charade you made last night extempore at Mrs. Drowzie's *conversazione.* Come now; your first is the name of a fish, your second a great naval commander, and——

Sir Benjamin. Uncle, now—prithee——

Crabtree. I'faith, ma'am, 'twould surprise you to hear how ready he is at all these sort of things.

Lady Sneerwell. I wonder, Sir Benjamin, you never publish anything.

Sir Benjamin. To say truth, ma'am, 'tis very vulgar to print; and, as my little productions are mostly satires and lampoons on particular people, I find they circulate more by giving copies in confidence to the friends of the parties. However, I have some love elegies, which, when favored with this lady's smiles, I mean to give the public.

Crabtree. (*To* MARIA.) 'Fore heaven, ma'am, they'll immortalize you—you will be handed down to posterity like Petrarch's Laura,[7] or Waller's Sacharissa.

Sir Benjamin. (*To* MARIA.) Yes, madam, I think you will like them when you shall see them on a beautiful quarto page, where a neat rivulet of text shall meander through a meadow of margin. 'Fore gad, they will be the most elegant things of their kind!

Crabtree. But, ladies, that's true—have you heard the news?

Mrs. Candour. What, sir, do you mean the report of—

Crabtree. No, ma'am, that's not it. Miss Nicely is going to be married to her own footman.

Mrs. Candour. Impossible!

Crabtree. Ask Sir Benjamin.

Sir Benjamin. 'Tis very true, ma'am: everything is fixed and the wedding liveries bespoke.

Crabtree. Yes—and they do say there were pressing reasons for it.

Lady Sneerwell. Why, I have heard something of this before.

Mrs. Candour. It can't be—and I wonder any one should believe such a story of so prudent a lady as Miss Nicely.

Sir Benjamin. O lud! ma'am, that's the very reason 'twas believed at once. She has always been so cautious and so reserved, that everybody was sure there was some reason for it at bottom.

Mrs. Candour. Why, to be sure, a tale of scandal is as fatal to the credit of a prudent lady of her stamp as a fever is generally to those of the strongest constitution. But there is a sort of puny, sickly reputation, that is always ailing, yet will outlive the robuster characters of a hundred prudes.

Sir Benjamin. True, madam, there are valetudinarians in reputation as well as constitution, who, being conscious of their weak part, avoid the least breath of air and supply their want of stamina by care and circumspection.

Mrs. Candour. Well, but this may be all a mistake. You know, Sir Benjamin, very trifling circumstances often give rise to the most injurious tales.

Crabtree. That they do, I'll be sworn, ma'am. Did you ever hear how Miss Piper came to lose her lover and her character last summer at Tunbridge? Sir Benjamin, you remember it?

Sir Benjamin. Oh, to be sure!—the most whimsical circumstance.

Lady Sneerwell. How was it, pray?

Crabtree. Why, one evening at Mrs. Ponto's assembly, the conversation happened to turn on the breeding of Nova Scotia sheep in this country. Says a young lady in company, "I have known instances of it; for Miss Letitia Piper, a first cousin of mine, had a Nova Scotia sheep that produced her twins." "What!" cries the Lady Dowager Dundizzy (who you know is as deaf as a post), "has Miss Piper had twins?" This mistake, as you may imagine, threw the whole company into a fit of laughter. However, 'twas the next morning everywhere reported, and in a few days believed by the whole town, that Miss Letitia Piper had actually been brought to bed of a fine boy and a girl: and in less than a week there were some people who could name the father, and the farm-house where the babies were put to nurse.

Lady Sneerwell. Strange, indeed!

Crabtree. Matter of fact, I assure you. O lud! Mr. Surface, pray is it true that your uncle, Sir Oliver, is coming home?

Joseph Surface. Not that I know of, indeed, sir.

Crabtree. He has been in the East Indies a long time. You can scarcely remember him, I believe? Sad comfort, whenever he returns, to hear how your brother has gone on!

Joseph Surface. Charles has been imprudent, sir, to be sure; but I hope no busy people have already prejudiced Sir Oliver against him. He may reform.

Sir Benjamin. To be sure he may. For my part I never believed him to be so utterly void of principle as people say; and though he has lost all his friends, I am told nobody is better spoken of by the Jews.

Crabtree. That's true, egad, nephew. If the old Jewry was a ward, I believe Charles would be an alderman: no man more popular there, 'fore gad! I hear he pays as many annuities as the Irish tontine;[8] and that whenever he is sick they have prayers for the recovery of his health in all the synagogues.

Sir Benjamin. Yet no man lives in greater splendor. They tell me, when he entertains his friends he will sit down to dinner with a dozen of his own securities, have a score of tradesmen in the ante-chamber, and an officer behind every guest's chair.

Joseph Surface. This may be entertainment to you, gentlemen, but you pay very little regard to the feelings of a brother.

Maria. (Aside.) Their malice is intolerable!—(*Aloud.*) Lady Sneerwell, I must wish you a good morning: I'm not very well.   *Exit.*

Mrs. Candour. O dear! she changes color very much.

Lady Sneerwell. Do, Mrs. Candour, follow her; she may want assistance.

Mrs. Candour. That I will, with all my soul, ma'am. Poor dear girl, who knows what her situation may be!   *Exit.*

Lady Sneerwell. 'Twas nothing but that she could not bear to hear Charles reflected on, notwithstanding their difference.

Sir Benjamin. The young lady's *penchant* is obvious.

Crabtree. But, Benjamin, you must not give up the pursuit for that: follow her and put her into good humor. Repeat her some of your own verses. Come, I'll assist you.

Sir Benjamin. Mr. Surface, I did not mean to hurt you; but depend on't your brother is utterly undone.

Crabtree. O lud, ay! undone as ever man was—can't raise a guinea!

Sir Benjamin. And everything sold, I'm told, that was movable.

Crabtree. I have seen one that was at his house. Not a thing left but some empty bottles that were overlooked and the family pictures which I believe are framed in the wainscots.

Sir Benjamin. And I'm very sorry also to hear some bad stories against him.

Crabtree. Oh, he has done many mean things, that's certain.

Sir Benjamin. But, however, as he's your brother——

(*Going.*)

Crabtree. We'll tell you all another opportunity.

Exeunt CRABTREE *and* SIR BENJAMIN.

Lady Sneerwell. Ha, ha! 'tis very hard for them to leave a subject they have not quite run down.

Joseph Surface. And I believe the abuse was no more acceptable to your ladyship than to Maria.

Lady Sneerwell. I doubt⁹ her affections are further engaged than we imagine. But the family are to be here this evening, so you may as well dine where you are and we shall have an opportunity of observing further. In the meantime, I'll go and plot mischief and you shall study sentiment. *Exeunt.*

SCENE II: SIR PETER TEAZLE'S *House.*

Enter SIR PETER

Sir Peter. When an old bachelor marries a young wife, what is he to expect? 'Tis now six months since Lady Teazle made me the happiest of men—and I have been the most miserable dog ever since! We tift a little going to church and fairly quarrelled before the bells had done ringing. I was more than once nearly choked with gall during the honeymoon, and had lost all comfort in life before my friends had done wishing me joy. Yet I chose with caution—a girl bred wholly in the country, who never knew luxury beyond one silk gown, nor dissipation above the annual gala of a race ball. Yet she now plays her part in all the extravagant fopperies of fashion and the town, with as ready a grace as if she never had seen a bush or a grass-plot out of Grosvenor Square! I am sneered at by all my acquaintance and paragraphed in the newspapers. She dissipates my fortune, and contradicts all my humors; yet the worst of it is, I doubt I love her, or I should never bear all this. However, I'll never be weak enough to own it.

Enter ROWLEY.

Rowley. Oh! Sir Peter, your servant: how is it with you, sir?

Sir Peter. Very bad, Master Rowley, very bad. I meet with nothing but crosses and vexations.

Rowley. What can have happened to trouble you since yesterday?

Sir Peter. A good question to a married man!

Rowley. Nay, I'm sure, Sir Peter, your lady can't be the cause of your uneasiness.

Sir Peter. Why, has anybody told you she was dead?

Rowley. Come, come, Sir Peter, you love her, notwithstanding your tempers don't exactly agree.

Sir Peter. But the fault is entirely hers, Master Rowley. I am myself the sweetest tempered man alive, and hate a teasing temper; and so I tell her a hundred times a day.

Rowley. Indeed!

Sir Peter. Ay; and what is very extraordinary, in all our disputes she is always in the wrong! But Lady Sneerwell and the set she meets at her house encourage the perverseness of her disposition. Then, to complete my vexation, Maria, my ward, whom I ought to have the power of a father over, is determined to turn rebel too and absolutely refuses the man whom I have long resolved on for her husband; meaning, I suppose, to bestow herself on his profligate brother.

Rowley. You know, Sir Peter, I have always taken the liberty to differ with you on the subject of these two young gentlemen. I only wish you may not be deceived in your opinion of the elder. For Charles, my life on't! he will retrieve his errors yet. Their worthy father, once my honored master, was, at his years, nearly as wild a spark; yet, when he died, he did not leave a more benevolent heart to lament his loss.

Sir Peter. You are wrong, Master Rowley. On their father's death, you know, I acted as a kind of guardian to them both till their uncle Sir Oliver's liberality gave them an early independence. Of course no person could have more opportunities of judging of their hearts, and I was never mistaken in my life. Joseph is indeed a model for the young men of the age. He is a man of sentiment and acts up to the sentiments he professes; but, for the other, take my word for't, if he had any grain of virtue by descent, he has dissipated it with the rest of his inheritance. Ah! my old friend Sir Oliver will be deeply mortified when he finds how part of his bounty has been misapplied.

Rowley. I am sorry to find you so violent against the young man, because this may be the most critical period of his fortune. I came hither with news that will surprise you.

Sir Peter. What! Let me hear.

Rowley. Sir Oliver is arrived, and at this moment in town.

Sir Peter. How! You astonish me! I thought you did not expect him this month.

Rowley. I did not: but his passage has been remarkably quick.

Sir Peter. Egad, I shall rejoice to see my old friend. 'Tis sixteen years since we met. We have had many a day together: but does he still enjoin us not to inform his nephews of his arrival?

Rowley. Most strictly. He means, before it is known, to make some trial of their dispositions.

Sir Peter. Ah! There needs no art to discover their merits—however, he shall have his way; but, pray, does he know I am married?

Rowley. Yes, and will soon wish you joy.

Sir Peter. What, as we drink health to a friend in consumption! Ah, Oliver will laugh at me. We used to rail at matrimony together, but he has been steady to his text. Well, he must be soon at my house, though—I'll instantly give orders for his reception. But, Master Rowley, don't drop a word that Lady Teazle and I ever disagree.

Rowley. By no means.

Sir Peter. For I should never be able to stand Noll's jokes; so I'll have him think, Lord forgive me! that we are a very happy couple.

Rowley. I understand you: but then you must be very careful not to differ while he is in the house with you.

Sir Peter. Egad, and so we must—and that's impossible. Ah! Master Rowley, when an old bachelor marries a young wife, he deserves—no—the crime carries its punishment along with it.   *Exeunt.*

ACT II

Scene I: Sir Peter Teazle's *House.*

Enter Sir Peter *and* Lady Teazle.

Sir Peter. Lady Teazle, Lady Teazle, I'll not bear it!

Lady Teazle. Sir Peter, Sir Peter, you may bear it or not as you please; but I ought to have my own way in everything,

and what's more, I will too. What though I was educated in
the country, I know very well that women of fashion in
London are accountable to nobody after they are married.

Sir Peter. Very well, ma'am, very well; so a husband is
to have no influence, no authority?

Lady Teazle. Authority! No, to be sure. If you wanted authority over me, you should have adopted me and not married
me: I am sure you were old enough.

Sir Peter. Old enough! ay, there it is! Well, well, Lady
Teazle, though my life may be made unhappy by your temper,
I'll not be ruined by your extravagance!

Lady Teazle. My extravagance! I'm sure I am not more extravagant than a woman of fashion ought to be.

Sir Peter. No, no, madam, you shall throw away no more
sums of such unmeaning luxury. 'Slife! to spend as much to
furnish your dressing-room with flowers in winter as would
suffice to turn the Pantheon[10] into a greenhouse, and give a
fête champêtre [11] at Christmas.

Lady Teazle. And am I to blame, Sir Peter, because flowers
are dear in cold weather? You should find fault with the
climate, and not with me. For my part, I'm sure I wish it
was spring all the year round and that roses grew under our
feet!

Sir Peter. Oons! madam—if you had been born to this, I
shouldn't wonder at your talking thus; but you forget what
your situation was when I married you.

Lady Teazle. No, no, I don't; 'twas a very disagreeable
one, or I should never have married you.

Sir Peter. Yes, yes, madam, you were then in somewhat a
humbler style—the daughter of a plain country squire. Recollect, Lady Teazle, when I saw you first sitting at your
tambour[12] in a pretty figured linen gown with a bunch of
keys at your side, your hair combed smooth over a roll and
your apartment hung round with fruits in worsted of your
own working.

Lady Teazle. Oh yes! I remember it very well, and a
curious life I led. My daily occupation to inspect the dairy,
superintend the poultry, make extracts from the family re-
ceipt-book, and comb my aunt Deborah's lapdog.

Sir Peter. Yes, yes, ma'am, 'twas so indeed.

Lady Teazle. And then, you know, my evening amusements!
To draw patterns for ruffles, which I had not the materials
to make up; to play Pope Joan[13] with the Curate; to read a
sermon to my aunt; or to be stuck down to an old spinet to
strum my father to sleep after a fox-chase.

Sir Peter. I am glad you have so good a memory. Yes,
madam, these were the recreations I took you from; but now

you must have your coach—*vis-à-vis*[14]—and three powdered footmen before your chair; and, in the summer, a pair of white cats[15] to draw you to Kensington Gardens. No recollection, I suppose, when you were content to ride double, behind the butler, on a docked coach-horse?

Lady Teazle. No—I swear I never did that; I deny the butler and the coach-horse.

Sir Peter. This, madam, was your situation; and what have I done for you? I have made you a woman of fashion, of fortune, of rank—in short, I have made you my wife.

Lady Teazle. Well, then, and there is but one thing more you can make me to add to the obligation, that is——

Sir Peter. My widow, I suppose?

Lady Teazle. Hem! hem!

Sir Peter. I thank you, madam—but don't flatter yourself; for, though your ill-conduct may disturb my peace it shall never break my heart, I promise you. However, I am equally obliged to you for the hint.

Lady Teazle. Then why will you endeavor to make yourself so disagreeable to me and thwart me in every little elegant expense?

Sir Peter. 'Slife, madam, I say; had you any of these little elegant expenses when you married me?

Lady Teazle. Lud, Sir Peter! would you have me be out of the fashion?

Sir Peter. The fashion, indeed! what had you to do with the fashion before you married me?

Lady Teazle. For my part, I should think you would like to have your wife thought a woman of taste.

Sir Peter. Ay—there again—taste! Zounds! madam, you had no taste when you married me!

Lady Teazle. That's very true, indeed, Sir Peter! and, after having married you, I should never pretend to taste again, I allow. But now, Sir Peter, since we have finished our daily jangle, I presume I may go to my engagement at Lady Sneerwell's?

Sir Peter. Ay, there's another precious circumstance—a charming set of acquaintance you have made there!

Lady Teazle. Nay, Sir Peter, they are all people of rank and fortune and remarkably tenacious of reputation.

Sir Peter. Yes, egad, they are tenacious of reputation with a vengeance; for they don't choose anybody should have a character but themselves! Such a crew! Ah! many a wretch has rid on a hurdle who has done less mischief than these utterers of forged tales, coiners of scandal, and clippers of reputation.

Lady Teazle. What, would you restrain the freedom of speech?

Sir Peter. Ah! They have made you just as bad as any one of the society.

Lady Teazle. Why, I believe I do bear a part with a tolerable grace. But I vow I bear no malice against the people I abuse: when I say an ill natured thing, 'tis out of pure good humor; and I take it for granted they deal exactly in the same manner with me. But, Sir Peter, you know you promised to come to Lady Sneerwell's too.

Sir Peter. Well, well, I'll call in just to look after my own character.

Lady Teazle. Then, indeed, you must make haste after me or you'll be too late. So goodbye to ye. *Exit.*

Sir Peter. So—I have gained much by my intended expostulation! Yet with what a charming air she contradicts everything I say, and how pleasantly she shows her contempt for my authority! Well, though I can't make her love me, there is great satisfaction in quarrelling with her; and I think she never appears to such advantage as when she is doing everything in her power to plague me. *Exit.*

SCENE II: LADY SNEERWELL'S *House.*

LADY SNEERWELL, MRS. CANDOUR, CRABTREE, SIR BENJAMIN BACKBITE, *and* JOSEPH SURFACE.

Lady Sneerwell. Nay, positively, we will hear it.

Joseph Surface. Yes, yes, the epigram, by all means.

Sir Benjamin. O plague on't, uncle! 'tis mere nonsense.

Crabtree. No, no; 'fore gad, very clever for an extempore!

Sir Benjamin. But, ladies, you should be acquainted with the circumstance. You must know, that one day last week as Lady Betty Curricle was taking the dust in Hyde Park, in a sort of duodecimo phaeton, she desired me to write some verses on her ponies; upon which, I took out my pocketbook, and in one moment produced the following:—

> Sure never were seen two such beautiful ponies;
> Other horses are clowns, but these macaronies: [16]
> To give them this title I am sure can't be wrong.
> Their legs are so slim, and their tails are so long.

Crabtree. There, ladies, done in the smack of a whip, and on horseback too.

Joseph Surface. A very Phœbus mounted—indeed, Sir Benjamin!

Sir Benjamin. Oh dear, sir!—trifles—trifles.

Enter LADY TEAZLE *and* MARIA

Mrs. Candour. I must have a copy.

Lady Sneerwell. Lady Teazle, I hope we shall see Sir Peter?

Lady Teazle. I believe he'll wait on your ladyship presently.

Lady Sneerwell. Maria, my love, you look grave. Come, you shall sit down to piquet with Mr. Surface.

Maria. I take very little pleasure in cards—however, I'll do as your ladyship pleases.

Lady Teazle. (*Aside.*) I am surprised Mr. Surface should sit down with her; I thought he would have embraced this opportunity of speaking to me before Sir Peter came.

Mrs. Candour. Now, I'll die; but you are so scandalous, I'll forswear your society.

Lady Teazle. What's the matter, Mrs. Candour?

Mrs. Candour. They'll not allow our friend Miss Vermillion to be handsome.

Lady Sneerwell. Oh, surely she is a pretty woman.

Crabtree. I am very glad you think so, ma'am.

Mrs. Candour. She has a charming fresh color.

Lady Teazle. Yes, when it is fresh put on.

Mrs. Candour. Oh, fie! I'll swear her color is natural: I have seen it come and go!

Lady Teazle. I dare swear you have, ma'am: it goes off at night and comes again in the morning.

Sir Benjamin. True, ma'am, it not only comes and goes; but, what's more, egad, her maid can fetch and carry it!

Mrs. Candour. Ha! ha! ha! how I hate to hear you talk so! But surely, now, her sister is, or was, very handsome.

Crabtree. Who? Mrs. Evergreen? O Lord! she's six-and-fifty if she's an hour!

Mrs. Candour. Now positively you wrong her; fifty-two or fifty-three is the utmost—and I don't think she looks more.

Sir Benjamin. Ah! there's no judging by her looks, unless one could see her face.

Lady Sneerwell. Well, well, if Mrs. Evergreen does take some pains to repair the ravages of time, you must allow she effects it with great ingenuity; and surely that's better than the careless manner in which the widow Ochre caulks her wrinkles.

Sir Benjamin. Nay, now, Lady Sneerwell, you are severe upon the widow. Come, come, 'tis not that she paints so ill —but, when she has finished her face, she joins it on so badly to her neck, that she looks like a mended statue, in which the connoisseur may see at once that the head's modern, though the trunk's antique!

Crabtree. Ha! ha! ha! Well said, nephew!

Mrs. Candour. Ha! ha! ha! Well, you make me laugh; but I vow I hate you for it. What do you think of Miss Simper?

Sir Benjamin. Why, she has very pretty teeth.

Lady Teazle. Yes; and on that account, when she is neither speaking nor laughing (which very seldom happens), she never absolutely shuts her mouth, but leaves it always on ajar, as it were—thus. (*Shows her teeth.*)

Mrs. Candour. How can you be so ill natured?

Lady Teazle. Nay, I allow even that's better than the pains Mrs. Prim takes to conceal her losses in front. She draws her mouth till it positively resembles the aperture of a poor's-box, and all her words appear to slide out edgewise, as it were—thus: *How do you do, madam? Yes, madam.*

Lady Sneerwell. Very well, Lady Teazle; I see you can be a little severe.

Lady Teazle. In defence of a friend it is but justice. But here comes Sir Peter to spoil our pleasantry.

Enter SIR PETER.

Sir Peter. Ladies, your most obedient—(*Aside.*) Mercy on me, here is the whole set! a character dead at every word, I suppose.

Mrs. Candour. I am rejoiced you are come, Sir Peter. They have been so censorious—and Lady Teazle as bad as any one.

Sir Peter. That must be very distressing to you, Mrs. Candour, I dare swear.

Mrs. Candour. Oh, they will allow good qualities to nobody; not even good nature to our friend Mrs. Pursy.

Lady Teazle. What, the fat dowager who was at Mrs. Quadrille's last night.

Mrs. Candour. Nay, her bulk is her misfortune; and, when she takes so much pains to get rid of it, you ought not to reflect on her.

Lady Sneerwell. That's very true, indeed.

Lady Teazle. Yes, I know she almost lives on acids and small whey; laces herself by pulleys; and often, in the hottest noon in summer, you may see her on a little squat pony, with her hair plaited up behind like a drummer's and puffing round the Ring[17] on a full trot.

Mrs. Candour. I thank you, Lady Teazle, for defending her.

Sir Peter. Yes, a good defence, truly.

Mrs. Candour. Truly, Lady Teazle is as censorious as Miss Sallow.

Crabtree. Yes, and she is a curious being to pretend to be censorious—an awkward gawky, without any one good point under heaven.

Mrs. Candour. Positively you shall not be so very severe. Miss Sallow is a near relation of mine by marriage, and, as for her person, great allowance is to be made; for, let me tell you, a woman labors under many disadvantages who tries to pass for a girl of six-and-thirty.

Lady Sneerwell. Though, surely, she is handsome still—and for the weakness in her eyes, considering how much she reads by candlelight; it is not to be wondered at.

Mrs. Candour. True; and then as to her manner, upon my word, I think it is particularly graceful, considering she never had the least education; for you know her mother was a Welsh milliner, and her father a sugar-baker at Bristol.

Sir Benjamin. Ah! you are both of you too good natured!

Sir Peter. (*Aside.*) Yes, damned good natured! This their own relation! mercy on me!

Mrs. Candour. For my part, I own I cannot bear to hear a friend ill spoken of.

Sir Peter. No, to be sure.

Sir Benjamin. Oh! you are of a moral turn. Mrs. Candour and I can sit for an hour and hear Lady Stucco talk sentiment.

Lady Teazle. Nay, I vow Lady Stucco is very well with the dessert after dinner; for she's just like the French fruit[18] one cracks for mottoes—made up of paint and proverb.

Mrs. Candour. Well, I will never join in ridiculing a friend; and so I constantly tell my cousin Ogle, and you all know what pretensions she has to be critical on beauty.

Crabtree. Oh, to be sure! she has herself the oddest countenance that ever was seen; 'tis a collection of features from all the different countries of the globe.

Sir Benjamin. So she has, indeed—an Irish front——

Crabtree. Caledonian locks——

Sir Benjamin. Dutch nose——

Crabtree. Austrian lips——

Sir Benjamin. Complexion of a Spaniard——

Crabtree. And teeth *à la Chinoise*——

Sir Benjamin. In short, her face resembles a *table d'hôte* at Spa—where no two guests are of a nation——

Crabtree. Or a congress at the close of a general war—wherein all the members, even to her eyes, appear to have a different interest, and her nose and chin are the only parties likely to join issue.

Mrs. Candour. Ha! ha! ha!

Sir Peter. (*Aside.*) Mercy on my life!—a person they dine with twice a week!

Lady Sneerwell. Go—go—you are a couple of provoking toads.

Mrs. Candour. Nay, but I vow you shall not carry the laugh off so—for give me leave to say, that Mrs. Ogle——

Sir Peter. Madam, madam, I beg your pardon—there's no stopping these good gentlemen's tongues. But when I tell you, Mrs. Candour, that the lady they are abusing is a particular friend of mine, I hope you'll not take her part.

Lady Sneerwell. Ha! ha! ha! well said, Sir Peter! but you are a cruel creature—too phlegmatic yourself for a jest, and too peevish to allow wit in others.

Sir Peter. Ah, madam, true wit is more nearly allied to good nature than your ladyship is aware of.

Lady Teazle. True, Sir Peter: I believe they are so near akin that they can never be united.

Sir Benjamin. Or rather, madam, I suppose them man and wife because one seldom sees them together.

Lady Teazle. But Sir Peter is such an enemy to scandal, I believe he would have it put down by Parliament.

Sir Peter. 'Fore heaven, madam, if they were to consider the sporting with reputation of as much importance as poaching on manors, and pass an act for the preservation of fame, I believe many would thank them for the bill.

Lady Sneerwell. O Lud! Sir Peter; would you deprive us of our privileges?

Sir Peter. Ay, madam; and then no person should be permitted to kill characters and run down reputations, but qualified old maids and disappointed widows.

Lady Sneerwell. Go, you monster!

Mrs. Candour. But, surely, you would not be quite so severe on those who only report what they hear?

Sir Peter. Yes, madam, I would have law merchant[19] for them too; and in all cases of slander currency, whenever the drawer of the lie was not to be found, the injured parties should have a right to come on any of the indorsers.

Crabtree. Well, for my part, I believe there never was a scandalous tale without some foundation.

Lady Sneerwell. Come, ladies, shall we sit down to cards in the next room?

Enter SERVANT, *who whispers* SIR PETER.

Sir Peter. I'll be with them directly.—(*Exit* SERVANT.) (*Aside.*) I'll get away unperceived.

Lady Sneerwell. Sir Peter, you are not going to leave us?

Sir Peter. Your ladyships must excuse me: I'm called away by particular business. But I leave my character behind me.
Exit.

Sir Benjamin. Well—certainly, Lady Teazle, that lord of yours is a strange being. I could tell you some stories of him would make you laugh heartily if he were not your husband.

Lady Teazle. Oh, pray don't mind that; come, do let's hear them.   (*Exeunt all but* JOSEPH SURFACE *and* MARIA.)

Joseph Surface. Maria, I see you have no satisfaction in this society.

Maria. How is it possible I should? If to raise malicious smiles at the infirmities or misfortunes of those who have never injured us be the province of wit or humor, Heaven grant me a double portion of dullness!

Joseph Surface. Yet they appear more ill natured than they are; they have no malice at heart.

Maria. Then is their conduct still more contemptible; for, in my opinion, nothing could excuse the intemperance of their tongues but a natural and uncontrollable bitterness of mind.

Joseph Surface. Undoubtedly, madam; and it has always been a sentiment of mine that to propagate a malicious truth wantonly is more despicable than to falsify from revenge. But can you, Maria, feel thus for others, and be unkind to me alone? Is hope to be denied the tenderest passion?

Maria. Why will you distress me by renewing this subject?

Joseph Surface. Ah, Maria! you would not treat me thus, and oppose your guardian, Sir Peter's will, but that I see that profligate Charles is still a favored rival.

Maria. Ungenerously urged! But whatever my sentiments are for that unfortunate young man, be assured I shall not feel more bound to give him up, because his distresses have lost him the regard even of a brother.

Joseph Surface. Nay, but, Maria, do not leave me with a frown: by all that's honest, I swear——   (*Kneels.*)

Enter LADY TEAZLE.

(*Aside.*) Gad's life, here's Lady Teazle.—(*Aloud to* MARIA.) You must not—no, you shall not—for, though I have the greatest regard for Lady Teazle——

Maria. Lady Teazle!

Joseph Surface. Yet were Sir Peter to suspect——

Lady Teazle. (*Coming forward.*) What is this, pray? Do you take her for me?—Child, you are wanted in the next room.—(*Exit* MARIA.) What is all this, pray?

Joseph Surface. Oh, the most unlucky circumstance in nature! Maria has somehow suspected the tender concern I have for your happiness, and threatened to acquaint Sir Peter with her suspicions, and I was just endeavoring to reason with her when you came in.

Lady Teazle. Indeed! but you seemed to adopt a very tender mode of reasoning—do you usually argue on your knees?

Joseph Surface. Oh, she's a child and I thought a little bombast——but, Lady Teazle, when are you to give me your judgment on my library, as you promised?

Lady Teazle. No, no; I begin to think it would be imprudent, and you know I admit you as a lover no farther than fashion requires.

Joseph Surface.—True—a mere Platonic *cicisbeo*,[20] what every wife is entitled to.

Lady Teazle. Certainly, one must not be out of the fashion. However, I have so many of my country prejudices left that, though Sir Peter's ill humor may vex me ever so, it never shall provoke me to——

Joseph Surface. The only revenge in your power. Well, I applaud your moderation.

Lady Teazle. Go—you are an insinuating wretch! But we shall be missed—let us join the company.

Joseph Surface. But we had best not return together.

Lady Teazle. Well, don't stay; for Maria shan't come to hear any more of your reasoning, I promise you.   *Exit.*

Joseph Surface. A curious dilemma, truly, my politics have run me into! I wanted, at first, only to ingratiate myself with Lady Teazle, that she might not be my enemy with Maria; and I have, I don't know how, become her serious lover. Sincerely I begin to wish I had never made such a point of gaining so very good a character; for it has led me into so many cursed rogueries that I doubt I shall be exposed at last.
    Exit.

SCENE III: SIR PETER TEAZLE'S *House.*

Enter SIR OLIVER SURFACE *and* ROWLEY.

Sir Oliver. Ha! ha! ha! so my old friend is married, hey? —a young wife out of the country. Ha! ha! ha! that he should have stood bluff[21] to old bachelor so long and sink into a husband at last!

Rowley. But you must not rally him on the subject, Sir Oliver; 'tis a tender point, I assure you, though he has been married only seven months.

Sir Oliver. Then he has been just half a year on the stool of repentance!—Poor Peter! But you say he has entirely given up Charles—never sees him, hey?

Rowley. His prejudice against him is astonishing, and I am sure greatly increased by a jealousy of him with Lady Teazle,

which he has industriously been led into by a scandalous
society in the neighborhood, who have contributed not a
little to Charles's ill name. Whereas the truth is, I believe, if
the lady is partial to either of them, his brother is the
favorite.

Sir Oliver. Ay, I know there are a set of malicious, prating,
prudent gossips, both male and female, who murder characters to kill time, and will rob a young fellow of his good
name before he has years to know the value of it. But I am
not to be prejudiced against my nephew by such, I promise
you! No, no; if Charles has done nothing false or mean, I
shall compound for his extravagance.

Rowley. Then, my life on't, you will reclaim him. Ah, sir,
it gives me new life to find that your heart is not turned
against him, and that the son of my good old master has
one friend, however, left.

Sir Oliver. What! shall I forget, Master Rowley, when I
was at his years myself? Egad, my brother and I were neither
of us very prudent youths; and yet, I believe, you have not
seen many better men than your old master was?

Rowley. Sir, 'tis this reflection gives me assurance that
Charles may yet be a credit to his family. But here comes
Sir Peter.

Sir Oliver. Egad, so he does! Mercy on me, he's greatly
altered, and seems to have a settled married look! One may
read *husband* in his face at this distance!

Enter SIR PETER.

Sir Peter. Ha! Sir Oliver—my old friend! Welcome to England a thousand times!

Sir Oliver. Thank you, thank you, Sir Peter! and i'faith I
am glad to find you well, believe me!

Sir Peter. Oh! 'tis a long time since we met—fifteen
years, I doubt, Sir Oliver, and many a cross accident in the
time.

Sir Oliver. Ay, I have had my share. But, what! I find you
are married, hey, my old boy? Well, well, it can't be helped;
and so—I wish you joy with all my heart!

Sir Peter. Thank you, thank you, Sir Oliver.—Yes, I have
entered into—the happy state; but we'll not talk of that now.

Sir Oliver. True, true, Sir Peter; old friends should not
begin on grievances at first meeting. No, no, no.

Rowley. (*Aside to* SIR OLIVER.) Take care, pray, sir.

Sir Oliver. Well, so one of my nephews is a wild rogue,
hey?

Sir Peter. Wild! Ah! my old friend, I grieve for your

disappointment there; he's a lost young man, indeed. However, his brother will make you amends; Joseph is, indeed, what a youth should be—everybody in the world speaks well of him.

Sir Oliver. I am sorry to hear it; he has too good a character to be an honest fellow. Everybody speaks well of him! Psha! then he has bowed as low to knaves and fools as to the honest dignity of genius and virtue.

Sir Peter. What, Sir Oliver! do you blame him for not making enemies?

Sir Oliver. Yes, if he has merit enough to deserve them.

Sir Peter. Well, well—you'll be convinced when you know him. 'Tis edification to hear him converse; he professes the noblest sentiments.

Sir Oliver. Oh, plague of his sentiments! If he salutes me with a scrap of morality in his mouth, I shall be sick directly. But, however, don't mistake me, Sir Peter; I don't mean to defend Charles's errors: but, before I form my judgment of either of them, I intend to make a trial of their hearts; and my friend Rowley and I have planned something for the purpose.

Rowley. And Sir Peter shall own for once he has been mistaken.

Sir Peter. Oh, my life on Joseph's honor!

Sir Oliver. Well—come, give us a bottle of good wine, and we'll drink the lads' health and tell you our scheme.

Sir Peter. Allons, then!

Sir Oliver. And don't, Sir Peter, be so severe against your old friend's son. Odds my life! I am not sorry that he has run out of the course a little. For my part, I hate to see prudence clinging to the green suckers of youth; 'tis like ivy round a sapling, and spoils the growth of the tree.   *Exeunt.*

ACT III

Scene I: Sir Peter Teazle's *House.*

Enter Sir Peter Teazle, Sir Oliver Surface, *and* Rowley.

Sir Peter. Well, then, we will see this fellow first and have our wine afterwards. But how is this, Master Rowley? I don't see the jet of your scheme.

Rowley. Why, sir, this Mr. Stanley, whom I was speaking of, is nearly related to them by their mother. He was once a merchant in Dublin, but has been ruined by a series of undeserved misfortunes. He has applied, by letter, since his confinement, both to Mr. Surface and Charles. From the former he has received nothing but evasive promises of future service, while Charles has done all that his extravagance has left him power to do; and he is, at this time, endeavoring to raise a sum of money, part of which, in the midst of his own distresses, I know he intends for the service of poor Stanley.

Sir Oliver. Ah, he is my brother's son.

Sir Peter. Well, but how is Sir Oliver personally to——

Rowley. Why, sir, I will inform Charles and his brother that Stanley has obtained permission to apply personally to his friends; and, as they have neither of them ever seen him, let Sir Oliver assume his character, and he will have a fair opportunity of judging, at least, of the benevolence of their dispositions; and believe me, sir, you will find in the youngest brother one who, in the midst of folly and dissipation, has still, as our immortal bard expresses it,—

a tear for pity, and a hand
Open as day, for melting charity.[22]

Sir Peter. Psha! What signifies his having an open hand or purse either, when he has nothing left to give? Well, well, make the trial, if you please. But where is the fellow whom you brought for Sir Oliver to examine relative to Charles's affairs?

Rowley. Below, waiting his commands, and no one can give him better intelligence.—This, Sir Oliver, is a friendly Jew, who, to do him justice, has done everything in his power to bring your nephew to a proper sense of his extravagance.

Sir Peter. Pray let us have him in.

Rowley. (*Calls to* SERVANT.) Desire Mr. Moses to walk upstairs.

Sir Peter. But, pray, why should you suppose he will speak the truth?

Rowley. Oh, I have convinced him that he has no chance of recovering certain sums advanced to Charles but through the bounty of Sir Oliver, who he knows is arrived; so that you may depend on his fidelity to his own interests. I have also another evidence in my power, one Snake, whom I have detected in a matter little short of forgery and shall shortly produce to remove some of your prejudices, Sir Peter, relative to Charles and Lady Teazle.

Sir Peter. I have heard too much on that subject.

Rowley. Here comes the honest Israelite.

Enter MOSES.

—This is Sir Oliver.

Sir Oliver. Sir, I understand you have lately had great dealings with my nephew Charles.

Moses. Yes, Sir Oliver, I have done all I could for him; but he was ruined before he came to me for assistance.

Sir Oliver. That was unlucky, truly; for you have had no opportunity of showing your talents.

Moses. None at all; I hadn't the pleasure of knowing his distresses till he was some thousands worse than nothing.

Sir Oliver. Unfortunate, indeed! But I suppose you have done all in your power for him, honest Moses?

Moses. Yes, he knows that. This very evening I was to have brought him a gentleman from the city, who does not know him, and will, I believe, advance him some money.

Sir Peter. What, one Charles has never had money from before?

Moses. Yes, Mr. Premium, of Crutched Friars, formerly a broker.

Sir Peter. Egad, Sir Oliver, a thought strikes me!—Charles, you say, does not know Mr. Premium?

Moses. Not at all.

Sir Peter. Now then, Sir Oliver, you may have a better opportunity of satisfying yourself than by an old romancing tale of a poor relation. Go with my friend Moses and represent Premium, and then, I'll answer for it, you'll see your nephew in all his glory.

Sir Oliver. Egad, I like this idea better than the other and I may visit Joseph afterwards as old Stanley.

Sir Peter. True—so you may.

Rowley. Well, this is taking Charles rather at a disadvantage, to be sure. However, Moses, you understand Sir Peter, and will be faithful.

Moses. You may depend upon me.—This is near the time I was to have gone.

Sir Oliver. I'll accompany you as soon as you please, Moses——But hold! I have forgot one thing—how the plague shall I be able to pass for a Jew?

Moses. There's no need—the principal is Christian.

Sir Oliver. Is he? I'm very sorry to hear it. But, then again, an't I rather too smartly dressed to look like a money-lender?

Sir Peter. Not at all; 'twould not be out of character, if you went in your carriage—would it, Moses?

Moses. Not in the least.

Sir Oliver. Well, but how must I talk? there's certainly

some cant of usury and mode of treating that I ought to know.

Sir Peter. Oh, there's not much to learn. The great point, as I take it, is to be exorbitant enough in your demands. Hey, Moses?

Moses. Yes, that's a very great point.

Sir Oliver. I'll answer for't I'll not be wanting in that. I'll ask him eight or ten per cent. on the loan, at least.

Moses. If you ask him no more than that, you'll be discovered immediately.

Sir Oliver. Hey! what, the plague! how much then?

Moses. That depends upon the circumstances. If he appears not very anxious for the supply, you should require only forty or fifty per cent.; but if you find him in great distress, and wanting the moneys very bad, you may ask double.

Sir Peter. A good honest trade you're learning, Sir Oliver!

Sir Oliver. Truly I think so—and not unprofitable.

Moses. Then, you know, you haven't the moneys yourself, but are forced to borrow them for him of a friend.

Sir Oliver. Oh! I borrow it of a friend, do I?

Moses. And your friend is an unconscionable dog: but you can't help that.

Sir Oliver. My friend an unconscionable dog, is he?

Moses. Yes, and he himself has not the moneys by him, but is forced to sell stocks at a great loss.

Sir Oliver. He is forced to sell stocks at a great loss, is he? Well, that's very kind of him.

Sir Peter. I'faith, Sir Oliver—Mr. Premium, I mean—you'll soon be master of the trade. But, Moses! would not you have him run out a little against the Annuity Bill?[23] That would be in character, I should think.

Moses. Very much.

Rowley. And lament that a young man now must be at years of discretion before he is suffered to ruin himself?

Moses. Ay, great pity!

Sir Peter. And abuse the public for allowing merit to an act whose only object is to snatch misfortune and imprudence from the rapacious grip of usury, and give the minor a chance of inheriting his estate without being undone by coming into possession.

Sir Oliver. So, so—Moses shall give me further instructions as we go together.

Sir Peter. You will not have much time, for your nephew lives hard by.

Sir Oliver. Oh, never fear! my tutor appears so able, that though Charles lived in the next street, it must be my own

fault if I am not a complete rogue before I turn the corner.
(*Exit with* MOSES.)

Sir Peter. So, now, I think Sir Oliver will be convinced;
you are partial, Rowley, and would have prepared Charles
for the other plot.

Rowley. No, upon my word, Sir Peter.

Sir Peter. Well, go bring me this Snake, and I'll hear what
he has to say presently. I see Maria and want to speak with
her.—(*Exit* ROWLEY.) I should be glad to be convinced my
suspicions of Lady Teazle and Charles were unjust. I have
never yet opened my mind on this subject to my friend
Joseph—I am determined I will do it—he will give me his
opinion sincerely.

Enter MARIA

So, child, has Mr. Surface returned with you?

Maria. No, sir; he was engaged.

Sir Peter. Well, Maria, do you not reflect, the more you
converse with that amiable young man, what return his partiality for you deserves?

Maria. Indeed, Sir Peter, your frequent importunity on
this subject distresses me extremely—you compel me to declare, that I know no man who has ever paid me a particular
attention whom I would not prefer to Mr. Surface.

Sir Peter. So—here's perverseness! No, no, Maria, 'tis
Charles only whom you would prefer. 'Tis evident his vices
and follies have won your heart.

Maria. This is unkind, sir. You know I have obeyed you
in neither seeing nor corresponding with him: I have heard
enough to convince me that he is unworthy of my regard. Yet
I cannot think it culpable, if, while my understanding se-
verely condemns his vices, my heart suggests some pity for
his distresses.

Sir Peter. Well, well, pity him as much as you please; but
give your heart and hand to a worthier object.

Maria. Never to his brother!

Sir Peter. Go, perverse and obstinate! But take care, madam; you have never yet known what the authority of a
guardian is. Don't compel me to inform you of it.

Maria. I can only say, you shall not have just reason. 'Tis
true, by my father's will, I am for a short period bound to
regard you as his substitute; but must cease to think you so,
when you would compel me to be miserable.   *Exit.*

Sir Peter. Was ever man so crossed as I am, everything
conspiring to fret me! I had not been involved in matrimony

a fortnight, before her father, a hale and hearty man, died, on purpose, I believe, for the pleasure of plaguing me with the care of his daughter.—(LADY TEAZLE *sings without.*) But here comes my helpmate! She appears in great good humor. How happy I should be if I could tease her into loving me, though but a little!

Enter LADY TEAZLE.

Lady Teazle. Lud! Sir Peter, I hope you haven't been quarrelling with Maria? It is not using me well to be ill humored when I am not by.

Sir Peter. Ah, Lady Teazle, you might have the power to make me good humored at all times.

Lady Teazle. I am sure I wish I had; for I want you to be in a charming sweet temper at this moment. Do be good humored now, and let me have two hundred pounds, will you?

Sir Peter. Two hundred pounds; what, an't I to be in a good humor without paying for it! But speak to me thus, and i'faith there's nothing I could refuse you. You shall have it; but seal me a bond for the repayment.

Lady Teazle. Oh, no—there—my note of hand will do as well.   (*Offering her hand.*)

Sir Peter. And you shall no longer reproach me with not giving you an independent settlement. I mean shortly to surprise you; but shall we always live thus, hey?

Lady Teazle. If you please; I'm sure I don't care how soon we leave off quarrelling, provided you'll own you were tired first.

Sir Peter. Well—then let our future contest be, who shall be most obliging.

Lady Teazle. I assure you, Sir Peter, good nature becomes you. You look now as you did before we were married, when you used to walk with me under the elms, and tell me stories of what a gallant you were in your youth, and chuck me under the chin, you would; and ask me if I thought I could love an old fellow who would deny me nothing—didn't you?

Sir Peter. Yes, yes, and you were as kind and attentive—

Lady Teazle. Ay, so I was, and would always take your part, when my acquaintance used to abuse you, and turn you into ridicule.

Sir Peter. Indeed!

Lady Teazle. Ay, and when my cousin Sophy has called you a stiff, peevish old bachelor, and laughed at me for thinking of marrying one who might be my father, I have always defended you, and said, I didn't think you so ugly by any means, and that I dared say you'd make a very good sort of a husband.

Sir Peter. And you prophesied right; and we shall now be the happiest couple——

Lady Teazle. And never differ again?

Sir Peter. No, never—though at the same time, indeed, my dear Lady Teazle, you must watch your temper very seriously; for in all our little quarrels, my dear, if you recollect, my love, you always began first.

Lady Teazle. I beg your pardon, my dear Sir Peter; indeed, you always gave the provocation.

Sir Peter. Now, see, my angel! take care—contradicting isn't the way to keep friends.

Lady Teazle. Then don't you begin it, my love!

Sir Peter. There, now! you—you are going on. You don't perceive, my life, that you are just doing the very thing which you know always makes me angry.

Lady Teazle. Nay, you know if you will be angry without any reason, my dear——

Sir Peter. There! now you want to quarrel again.

Lady Teazle. No, I'm sure I don't; but, if you will be so peevish——

Sir Peter. There now! who begins first?

Lady Teazle. Why, you, to be sure. I said nothing—but there's no bearing your temper.

Sir Peter. No, no madam: the fault's in your own temper.

Lady Teazle. Ay, you are just what my cousin Sophy said you would be.

Sir Peter. Your cousin Sophy is a forward, impertinent gipsy.

Lady Teazle. You are a great bear, I am sure, to abuse my relations.

Sir Peter. Now may all the plagues of marriage be doubled on me if ever I try to be friends with you any more!

Lady Teazle. So much the better.

Sir Peter. No, no, madam. 'Tis evident you never cared a pin for me, and I was a madman to marry you—a pert, rural coquette, that had refused half the honest 'squires in the neighborhood!

Lady Teazle. And I am sure I was a fool to marry you—an old dangling bachelor, who was single at fifty, only because he never could meet with any one who would have him.

Sir Peter. Ay, ay, madam; but you were pleased enough to listen to me: you never had such an offer before.

Lady Teazle. No! didn't I refuse Sir Tivy Terrier, who everybody said would have been a better match? for his estate is just as good as yours, and he has broke his neck since we have been married.

Sir Peter. I have done with you, madam! You are an unfeeling, ungrateful—but there's an end of everything. I believe you capable of everything that is bad. Yes, madam, I now believe the reports relative to you and Charles, madam. Yes, madam, you and Charles are, not without grounds——

Lady Teazle. Take care, Sir Peter! you had better not insinuate any such thing! I'll not be suspected without cause, I promise you.

Sir Peter. Very well, madam! very well! a separate maintenance as soon as you please. Yes, madam, or a divorce! I'll make an example of myself for the benefit of all old bachelors. Let us separate, madam.

Lady Teazle. Agreed! agreed! And now, my dear Sir Peter, we are of a mind once more, we may be the happiest couple, and never differ again, you know: ha! ha! ha! Well, you are going to be in a passion, I see, and I shall only interrupt you—so, bye! bye!   *Exit.*

Sir Peter. Plagues and tortures! can't I make her angry either! Oh, I am the most miserable fellow! But I'll not bear her presuming to keep her temper: no! she may break my heart, but she shan't keep her temper.   *Exit.*

SCENE II: CHARLES SURFACE'S *House.*

Enter TRIP, MOSES, *and* SIR OLIVER SURFACE.

Trip. Here, Master Moses! if you'll stay a moment; I'll try whether—what's the gentleman's name?

Sir Oliver. (*Aside to* MOSES.) Mr. Moses, what is my name?

Moses. Mr. Premium.

Trip. Premium—very well.   *Exit, taking snuff.*

Sir Oliver. To judge by the servants, one wouldn't believe the master was ruined. But what!—sure, this was my brother's house?

Moses. Yes, sir; Mr. Charles bought it of Mr. Joseph, with the furniture, pictures, &c., just as the old gentleman left it. Sir Peter thought it a piece of extravagance in him.

Sir Oliver. In my mind, the other's economy in selling it to him was more reprehensible by half.

Re-enter TRIP.

Trip. My master says you must wait, gentlemen: he has company, and can't speak with you yet.

Sir Oliver. If he knew who it was wanted to see him, perhaps he would not send such a message?

Trip. Yes, yes, sir; he knows you are here—I did not forget little Premium: no, no, no.

Sir Oliver. Very well; and I pray, sir, what may be your name?

Trip. Trip, sir; my name is Trip, at your service.

Sir Oliver. Well, then, Mr. Trip, you have a pleasant sort of place here, I guess?

Trip. Why, yes—here are three or four of us to pass our time agreeably enough; but then our wages are sometimes a little in arrear—and not very great either—but fifty pounds a year, and find our own bags and bouquets.[24]

Sir Oliver. (*Aside.*) Bags and bouquets! halters and bastinadoes!

Trip. And *à propos*, Moses, have you been able to get me that little bill discounted?

Sir Oliver. (*Aside.*) Wants to raise money, too!—mercy on me! Has his distresses too, I warrant, like a lord, and affects creditors and duns.

Moses. 'Twas not to be done, indeed, Mr. Trip.

Trip. Good lack, you surprise me! My friend Brush has indorsed it, and I thought when he put his name at the back of a bill 'twas the same as cash.

Moses. No, 'twouldn't do.

Trip. A small sum—but twenty pounds. Hark'ee, Moses, do you think you couldn't get it me by way of annuity?

Sir Oliver. (*Aside.*) An annuity! ha! ha! a footman raise money by way of annuity. Well done, luxury, egad!

Moses. Well, but you must insure your place.

Trip. Oh, with all my heart! I'll insure my place and my life too, if you please.

Sir Oliver. (*Aside.*) It's more than I would your neck.

Moses. But is there nothing you could deposit?

Trip. Why, nothing capital of my master's wardrobe has dropped lately; but I could give you a mortgage on some of his winter clothes, with equity of redemption before November—or you shall have the revision of the French velvet, or a post-obit[25] on the blue and silver. These, I should think, Moses, with a few pair of point ruffles, as a collateral security—hey, my little fellow?

Moses. Well, well. (*Bell rings.*)

Trip. Egad. I heard the bell! I believe, gentlemen, I can now introduce you. Don't forget the annuity, little Moses! This way, gentlemen, I'll insure my place, you know.

Sir Oliver. (*Aside.*) If the man be a shadow of the master, this is the temple of dissipation indeed! *Exeunt.*

SCENE III: *Another Room.*

CHARLES SURFACE, CARELESS, &c., &c.,
at a table with wine, &c.

Charles Surface. 'Fore heaven, 'tis true! there's the great degeneracy of the age. Many of our acquaintance have taste, spirit, and politeness; but plague on't they won't drink.

Careless. It is so, indeed, Charles! they give in to all the substantial luxuries of the table, and abstain from nothing but wine and wit. Oh, certainly society suffers by it intolerably! for now, instead of the social spirit of raillery that used to mantle over a glass of bright Burgundy, their conversation is become just like the Spa-water they drink, which has all the pertness and flatulency of champagne, without its spirit or flavor.

1 Gent. But what are they to do who love play better than wine?

Careless. True! there's Sir Harry diets himself for gaming, and is now under a hazard regimen.

Charles Surface. Then he'll have the worst of it. What! you wouldn't train a horse for the course by keeping him from corn? For my part, egad, I'm never so successful as when I am a little merry. Let me throw on a bottle of champagne and I never lose—at least I never feel my losses, which is exactly the same thing.

2 Gent. Ay, that I believe.

Charles Surface. And then, what man can pretend to be a believer in love who is an abjurer of wine? 'Tis the test by which the lover knows his own heart. Fill a dozen bumpers to a dozen beauties, and she that floats at the top is the maid that bewitched you.

Careless. Now then, Charles, be honest, and give us your real favorite.

Charles Surface. Why, I have withheld her only in compassion to you. If I toast her, you must give her a round of her peers, which is impossible—on earth.

Careless. Oh, then we'll find some canonized vestals or heathen goddesses that will do, I warrant!

Charles Surface. Here then, bumpers, you rogues! bumpers! Maria! Maria—

Sir Toby. Maria who?

Charles Surface. Oh, damn the surname!—'tis too formal to be registered in Love's calendar—but now, Sir Toby, beware, we must have beauty superlative.

Careless. Nay, never study, Sir Toby: we'll stand to the

toast, though your mistress should want an eye, and you know you have a song will excuse you.

Sir Toby. Egad, so I have! and I'll give him the song instead of the lady. (*Sings.*)

> Here's to the maiden of bashful fifteen;
>   Here's to the widow of fifty;
> Here's to the flaunting extravagant quean,[26]
>   And here's to the housewife that's thrifty.

> *Chorus.*   Let the toast pass,
>   Drink to the lass,
> I'll warrant she'll prove an excuse for a glass!

> Here's to the charmer whose dimples we prize;
>   Now to the maid who has none, sir;
> Here's to the girl with a pair of blue eyes,
>   And here's to the nymph with but one, sir.

> *Chorus.*   Let the toast pass,
>   Drink to the lass,
> I'll warrant she'll prove an excuse for a glass.

> Here's to the maid with a bosom of snow;
>   Now to her that's as brown as a berry;
> Here's to the wife with a face full of woe,
>   And now to the damsel that's merry.

> *Chorus.*   Let the toast pass,
>   Drink to the lass,
> I'll warrant she'll prove an excuse for a glass.

> For let 'em be clumsy, or let 'em be slim,
>   Young or ancient, I care not a feather;
> So fill a pint bumper quite up to the brim,
>   And let us e'en toast them together.

> *Chorus.*   Let the toast pass,
>   Drink to the lass,
> I'll warrant she'll prove an excuse for a glass.

All. Bravo! Bravo!

Enter TRIP, *and whispers* CHARLES SURFACE.

Charles Surface. Gentlemen, you must excuse me a little. Careless, take the chair, will you?

Careless. Nay, prithee, Charles, what now? This is one of your peerless beauties, I suppose, has dropped in by chance?

Charles Surface. No, faith! To tell you the truth, 'tis a Jew and a broker, who are come by appointment.

Careless. Oh, damn it! let's have the Jew in.

1 Gent. Ay, and the broker too, by all means.

2 Gent. Yes, yes, the Jew and the broker!

Charles Surface. Egad, with all my heart!—Trip, bid the gentlemen walk in. (*Exit* TRIP.) Though there's one of them a stranger I can tell you.

Careless. Charles, let us give them some generous Burgundy and perhaps they'll grow conscientious.

Charles Surface. Oh, hang 'em, no! wine does but draw forth a man's natural qualities; and to make them drink would only be to whet their knavery.

Enter TRIP, *with* SIR OLIVER SURFACE *and* MOSES.

Charles Surface. So, honest Moses; walk in, pray, Mr. Premium—that's the gentleman's name, isn't it, Moses?

Moses. Yes, sir.

Charles Surface. Set chairs, Trip.—Sit down, Mr. Premium. Glasses, Trip.—Sit down, Moses.—Come, Mr. Premium, I'll give you a sentiment; here's *Success to usury!*—Moses, fill the gentleman a bumper.

Moses. Success to usury!   (*Drinks.*)

Careless. Right, Moses—usury is prudence and industry, and deserves to succeed.

Sir Oliver. Then here's—All the success it deserves!
                                                             (*Drinks.*)

Careless. No, no, that won't do! Mr. Premium, you have demurred at the toast, and must drink it in a pint bumper.

1 Gent. A pint bumper, at least!

Moses. Oh, pray, sir, consider—Mr. Premium's a gentleman.

Careless. And therefore loves good wine.

2 Gent. Give Moses a quart glass—this is mutiny, and a high contempt of the chair.

Careless. Here, now for't! I'll see justice done, to the last drop of my bottle.

Sir Oliver. Nay, pray, gentlemen—I did not expect this usage.

Charles Surface. No, hang it, you shan't; Mr. Premium's a stranger.

Sir Oliver. (*Aside.*) Odd! I wish I was well out of their company.

Careless. Plague on 'em then! if they won't drink, we'll not sit down with them. Come, Toby, the dice are in the next room.—Charles, you'll join us when you have finished your business with the gentlemen?

Charles Surface. I will! I will!—(*Exeunt* GENTLEMEN.) Careless!

Careless. (*Returning.*) Well?

Charles Surface. Perhaps I may want you.

Careless. Oh, you know I am always ready: word, note, or bond, 'tis all the same to me.   *Exit.*

Moses. Sir, this is Mr. Premium, a gentleman of the strictest honor and secrecy; and always performs what he undertakes. Mr. Premium, this is——

Charles Surface. Psha! have done. Sir, my friend Moses is a very honest fellow, but a little slow at expression: he'll be an hour giving us our titles. Mr. Premium, the plain state of the matter is this: I am an extravagant young fellow who wants to borrow money; you I take to be a prudent old fellow, who has got money to lend. I am blockhead enough to give fifty per cent sooner than not have it! and you, I presume, are rogue enough to take a hundred if you can get it. Now, sir, you see we are acquainted at once, and may proceed to business without further ceremony.

Sir Oliver. Exceeding frank, upon my word. I see, sir, you are not a man of many compliments.

Charles Surface. Oh, no, sir! plain dealing in business I always think best.

Sir Oliver. Sir, I like you the better for it. However, you are mistaken in one thing. I have no money to lend, but I believe I could procure some of a friend; but then he's an unconscionable dog. Isn't he, Moses? And must sell stock to accommodate you. Mustn't he, Moses?

Moses. Yes, indeed! You know I always speak the truth, and scorn to tell a lie!

Charles Surface. Right. People that speak truth generally do. But these are trifles, Mr. Premium. What! I know money isn't to be bought without paying for't!

Sir Oliver. Well, but what security could you give? You have no land, I suppose?

Charles Surface. Not a mole-hill, nor a twig, but what's in the bough-pots [27] out of the window!

Sir Oliver. Nor any stock, I presume?

Charles Surface. Nothing but live stock—and that's only a few pointers and ponies. But pray, Mr. Premium, are you acquainted at all with any of my connections?

Sir Oliver. Why, to say the truth, I am.

Charles Surface. Then you must know that I have a devilish rich uncle in the East Indies, Sir Oliver Surface, from whom I have the greatest expectations?

Sir Oliver. That you have a wealthy uncle, I have heard; but how your expectations will turn out is more, I believe, than you can tell.

Charles Surface. Oh, no!—there can be no doubt. They tell me I'm a prodigious favorite, and that he talks of leaving me everything.

Sir Oliver. Indeed! this is the first I've heard of it.

Charles Surface. Yes, yes, 'tis just so. Moses knows 'tis true; don't you, Moses?

Moses. Oh, yes! I'll swear to't.

Sir Oliver. (*Aside*.) Egad, they'll persuade me presently I'm at Bengal.

Charles Surface. Now I propose, Mr. Premium, if it's agreeable to you, a post-obit on Sir Oliver's life: though at the same time the old fellow has been so liberal with me, that I give you my word, I should be very sorry to hear that anything had happened to him.

Sir Oliver. Not more than I should, I assure you. But the bond you mention happens to be just the worst security you could offer me—for I might live to be a hundred and never see the principal.

Charles Surface. Oh, yes, you would! the moment Sir Oliver dies, you know, you would come on me for the money.

Sir Oliver. Then I believe I should be the most unwelcome dun you ever had in your life.

Charles Surface. What! I suppose you're afraid that Sir Oliver is too good a life?

Sir Oliver. No, indeed I am not; though I have heard he is as hale and healthy as any man of his years in Christendom.

Charles Surface. There again, now, you are misinformed. No, no, the climate has hurt him considerably, poor uncle Oliver. Yes, yes, he breaks apace, I'm told—and is so much altered lately that his nearest relations would not know him.

Sir Oliver. No! Ha! ha! ha! so much altered lately that his nearest relation would not know him! Ha! ha! ha! egad—ha! ha! ha!

Charles Surface. Ha! ha!—you're glad to hear that, little Premium.

Sir Oliver. No, no, I'm not.

Charles Surface. Yes, yes, you are—ha! ha! ha!—you know that mends your chance.

Sir Oliver. But I'm told Sir Oliver is coming over; nay, some say he has actually arrived.

Charles Surface. Psha! sure I must know better than you whether he's come or not. No, no, rely on't he's at this moment at Calcutta. Isn't he, Moses?

Moses. Oh, yes, certainly.

Sir Oliver. Very true, as you say, you must know better than I, though I have it from a pretty good authority. Haven't I, Moses?

Moses. Yes, most undoubted!

Sir Oliver. But, sir, as I understand you want a few hundreds immediately, is there nothing you could dispose of?

Charles Surface. How do you mean?

Sir Oliver. For instance, now, I have heard that your father left behind him a great quantity of massy old plate.

Charles Surface. O lud, that's gone long ago. Moses can tell you how better than I can.

Sir Oliver. (*Aside.*) Good lack! all the family race-cups and corporation-bowls! [28]—(*Aloud.*) Then it was also supposed that his library was one of the most valuable and compact.

Charles Surface. Yes, yes, so it was—vastly too much for a private gentleman. For my part, I was always of a communicative disposition, so I thought it a shame to keep so much knowledge to myself.

Sir Oliver. (*Aside.*) Mercy upon me! learning that had run in the family like an heirloom!—(*Aloud.*) Pray, what has become of the books?

Charles Surface. You must inquire of the auctioneer, Master Premium, for I don't believe even Moses can direct you.

Moses. I know nothing of books.

Sir Oliver. So, so, nothing of the family property left, I suppose?

Charles Surface. Not much, indeed; unless you have a mind to the family pictures. I have got a room full of ancestors above; and if you have a taste for old paintings, egad, you shall have 'em a bargain!

Sir Oliver. Hey! what the devil! sure, you wouldn't sell your forefathers, would you?

Charles Surface. Every man of them, to the best bidder.

Sir Oliver. What! your great-uncles and aunts?

Charles Surface. Ay, and my great-grandfathers and grandmothers too.

Sir Oliver. (*Aside.*) Now I give him up!—(*Aloud.*) What the plague, have you no bowels for your own kindred? Odd's

life! do you take me for Shylock in the play, that you would
raise money of me on your own flesh and blood?

Charles Surface. Nay, my little broker, don't be angry.
What need you care, if you have your money's worth?

Sir Oliver. Well, I'll be the purchaser. I think I can dispose of the family canvas.—(*Aside.*) Oh, I'll never forgive
him this! never!

Enter CARELESS.

Careless. Come, Charles, what keeps you?

Charles Surface. I can't come yet. I'faith, we are going to
have a sale above stairs; here's little Premium will buy all
my ancestors!

Careless. Oh, burn your ancestors!

Charles Surface. No, he may do that afterwards, if he
pleases. Stay, Careless, we want you: egad, you shall be
auctioneer—so come along with us.

Careless. Oh, have with you, if that's the case. I can
handle a hammer as well as a dice box!

Sir Oliver. (*Aside.*) Oh, the profligates!

Charles Surface. Come, Moses, you shall be appraiser, if
we want one. Gad's life, little Premium, you don't seem to
like the business!

Sir Oliver. Oh, yes, I do, vastly! Ha! ha! ha! yes, yes, I
think it a rare joke to sell one's family by auction—ha! ha!—
(*Aside.*) Oh, the prodigal!

Charles Surface. To be sure! when a man wants money,
where the plague should he get assistance if he can't make
free with his own relations?   *Exeunt.*

ACT IV

SCENE I: *Picture Room at* CHARLES'S.

Enter CHARLES SURFACE, SIR OLIVER SURFACE, MOSES, *and* CARELESS.

Charles Surface. Walk in, gentlemen, pray walk in;—
here they are, the family of the Surfaces up to the Conquest.

Sir Oliver. And, in my opinion, a goodly collection.

Charles Surface. Ay, ay, these are done in the true spirit
of portrait-painting; no *volontière grace* or expression. Not
like the works of your modern Raphaels, who give you the

strongest resemblance, yet contrive to make your portrait independent of you; so that you may sink the original and not hurt the picture. No, no; the merit of these is the inveterate likeness—all stiff and awkward as the originals, and like nothing in human nature besides.

Sir Oliver. Ah! we shall never see such figures of men again.

Charles Surface. I hope not. Well, you see, Master Premium, what a domestic character I am; here I sit of an evening surrounded by my family. But come, get to your pulpit, Mr. Auctioneer; here's an old gouty chair of my grandfather's will answer the purpose.

Careless. Ay, ay, this will do. But, Charles, I haven't a hammer; and what's an auctioneer without his hammer?

Charles Surface. Egad, that's true. What parchment have we here? Oh, our geneaology in full. Here, Careless, you shall have no common bit of mahogany, here's the family tree for you, you rogue! This shall be your hammer, and now you may knock down my ancestors with their own pedigree.

Sir Oliver. (*Aside.*) What an unnatural rogue!—an *ex post facto* parricide!

Careless. Yes, yes, here's a list of your generation indeed; —faith, Charles, this is the most convenient thing you could have found for the business, for 'twill not only serve as a hammer, but a catalogue into the bargain. Come, begin— A-going, a-going, a-going!

Charles Surface. Bravo, Careless! Well, here's my great uncle, Sir Richard Raveline, a marvellous good general in his day, I assure you. He served in all the Duke of Marlborough's wars, and got that cut over his eye at the battle of Malplaquet.[29] What say you, Mr. Premium? look at him—there's a hero! not cut out of his feathers, as your modern clipped captains are, but enveloped in wig and regimentals as a general should be. What do you bid?

Moses. Mr. Premium would have you speak.

Charles Surface. Why, then, he shall have him for ten pounds, and I'm sure that's not dear for a staff-officer.

Sir Oliver. (*Aside.*) Heaven deliver me! his famous uncle Richard for ten pounds!—(*Aloud.*) Very well, sir, I take him at that.

Charles Surface. Careless, knock down my uncle Richard. —Here, now, is a maiden sister of his, my great-aunt Deborah, done by Kneller,[30] in his best manner, and a very formidable likeness. There she is, you see, a shepherdess feeding her flock. You shall have her for five pounds ten— the sheep are worth the money.

Sir Oliver. (*Aside.*) Ah! poor Deborah! a woman who set such a value on herself!—(*Aloud.*) Five pounds ten—she's mine.

Charles Surface. Knock down my aunt Deborah! Here, now, are two that were a sort of cousins of theirs.—You see, Moses, these pictures were done some time ago, when beaux wore wigs, and the ladies their own hair.

Sir Oliver. Yes, truly, head-dresses appear to have been a little lower in those days.

Charles Surface. Well, take that couple for the same.

Moses. 'Tis a good bargain.

Charles Surface. Careless!—This, now, is a grandfather of my mother's, a learned judge, well known on the western circuit.—What do you rate him at, Moses?

Moses. Four guineas.

Charles Surface. Four guineas! Gad's life, you don't bid me the price of his wig—Mr. Premium, you have more respect for the wool-sack;[31] do let us knock his Lordship down at fifteen.

Sir Oliver. By all means.

Careless. Gone!

Charles Surface. And there are two brothers of his, William and Walter Blunt, Esquires, both members of Parliament, and noted speakers; and, what's very extraordinary, I believe, this is the first time they were ever bought or sold.

Sir Oliver. That is very extraordinary, indeed! I'll take them at forty.

Charles Surface. Here's a jolly fellow—I don't know what relation, but he was mayor of Manchester: take him at eight pounds.

Sir Oliver. No, no; six will do for the mayor.

Charles Surface. Come, make it guineas, and I'll throw you the two aldermen there into the bargain.

Sir Oliver. They're mine.

Charles Surface. Careless, knock down the mayor and aldermen. But, plague on't! we shall be all day retailing in this manner; do let us deal wholesale: what say you, little Premium? Give me three hundred pounds for the rest of the family in the lump.

Careless. Ay ay, that will be the best way.

Sir Oliver. Well, well, anything to accommodate you; they are mine. But there is one portrait which you have always passed over.

Careless. What, that ill-looking little fellow over the settee?

Sir Oliver. Yes, sir, I mean that; though I don't think him so ill-looking a little fellow, by any means.

Charles Surface. What, that? Oh; that's my uncle Oliver! 'Twas done before he went to India.

Careless. Your uncle Oliver! Gad, then you'll never be friends, Charles. That, now, to me, is as stern a looking rogue as ever I saw; an unforgiving eye, and a damned disinheriting countenance! an inveterate knave, depend on't. Don't you think so, little Premium?

Sir Oliver. Upon my soul, sir, I do not; I think it is as honest a looking face as any in the room, dead or alive. But I suppose uncle Oliver goes with the rest of the lumber?

Charles Surface. No, hang it! I'll not part with poor Noll. The old fellow has been very good to me, and, egad, I'll keep his picture while I've a room to put it in.

Sir Oliver. (*Aside.*) The rogue's my nephew after all!— (*Aloud.*) But, sir, I have somehow taken a fancy to that picture.

Charles Surface. I'm sorry for't, for you certainly will not have it. Oons, haven't you got enough of them?

Sir Oliver. (*Aside.*) I forgive him everything!—(*Aloud.*) But, sir, when I take a whim in my head, I don't value money. I'll give you as much for that as for all the rest.

Charles Surface. Don't tease me, master broker; I tell you I'll not part with it, and there's an end of it.

Sir Oliver. (*Aside.*) How like his father the dog is!— (*Aloud.*) Well, well, I have done.—(*Aside.*) I did not perceive it before, but I think I never saw such a striking resemblance.—(*Aloud.*) Here is a draught for your sum.

Charles Surface. Why, 'tis for eight hundred pounds!

Sir Oliver. You will not let Sir Oliver go?

Charles Surface. Zounds! no! I tell you, once more.

Sir Oliver. Then never mind the difference, we'll balance that another time. But give me your hand on the bargain; you are an honest fellow, Charles—I beg pardon, sir, for being so free.—Come, Moses.

Charles Surface. Egad, this is a whimsical old fellow!— But hark'ee, Premium, you'll prepare lodgings for these gentlemen.

Sir Oliver. Yes, yes, I'll send for them in a day or two.

Charles Surface: But hold; do now send a genteel conveyance for them, for, I assure you, they were most of them used to ride in their own carriages.

Sir Oliver. I will, I will—for all but Oliver.

Charles Surface. Ay, all but the little nabob.

Sir Oliver. You're fixed on that?

Charles Surface. Peremptorily.

Sir Oliver. (*Aside.*) A dear extravagant rogue!—(*Aloud.*) Good day!—Come, Moses.—(*Aside.*) Let me hear now who dares call him profligate! *Exeunt* SIR OLIVER *and* MOSES.

Careless. Why, this is the oddest genius of the sort I ever met with!

Charles Surface. Egad, he's the prince of brokers, I think. I wonder how the devil Moses got acquainted with so honest a fellow.—Ha! here's Rowley.—Do, Careless, say I'll join the company in a few moments.

Careless. I will—but don't let that old blockhead persuade you to squander any of that money on old musty debts, or any such nonsense; for tradesmen, Charles, are the most exorbitant fellows.

Charles Surface. Very true, and paying them is only encouraging them.

Careless. Nothing else.

Charles Surface. Ay, ay, never fear.—(*Exit* CARELESS.) So! this was an odd old fellow, indeed. Let me see, two-thirds of this is mine by right: five hundred and thirty odd pounds. 'Fore heaven! I find one's ancestors are more valuable relations than I took them for!—Ladies and gentlemen, your most obedient and very grateful servant.

(*Bows to the pictures.*)

Enter ROWLEY.

Ha! old Rowley! egad, you are just come in time to take leave of your old acquaintance.

Rowley. Yes, I heard they were a-going. But I wonder you can have such spirits under so many distresses.

Charles Surface. Why, there's the point! my distresses are so many that I can't afford to part with my spirits; but I shall be rich and splenetic, all in good time. However, I suppose you are surprised that I am not more sorrowful at parting with so many near relations; to be sure, 'tis very affecting; but you see they never move a muscle, so why should I?

Rowley. There's no making you serious a moment.

Charles Surface. Yes, faith, I am so now. Here, my honest Rowley, here, get me this changed directly and take a hundred pounds of it immediately to old Stanley.

Rowley. A hundred pounds! Consider only——

Charles Surface. Gad's life, don't talk about it! poor Stanley's wants are pressing, and, if you don't make haste, we shall have some one call that has a better right to the money.

Rowley. Ah! there's the point! I never will cease dunning you with the old proverb——

Charles Surface. "Be just before you're generous."—Why, so I would if I could; but Justice is an old lame, hobbling beldame, and I can't get her to keep pace with Generosity, for the soul of me.

Rowley. Yet, Charles, believe me, one hour's reflection—
Charles Surface. Ay, ay, it's very true; but, hark'ee, Rowley, while I have, by Heaven I'll give; so, damn your economy! and now for hazard. *Exeunt.*

SCENE II: *The parlor.*

Enter SIR OLIVER SURFACE *and* MOSES.

Moses. Well, sir, I think, as Sir Peter said, you have seen Mr. Charles in high glory; 'tis great pity he's so extravagant.
Sir Oliver. True, but he would not sell my picture.
Moses. And loves wine and women so much.
Sir Oliver. But he would not sell my picture.
Moses. And games so deep.
Sir Oliver. But he would not sell my picture. Oh, here's Rowley.

Enter ROWLEY.

Rowley. So, Sir Oliver, I find you have made a purchase——
Sir Oliver. Yes, yes, our young rake has parted with his ancestors like old tapestry.
Rowley. And here has he commissioned me to re-deliver you part of the purchase-money—I mean, though, in your necessitous character of old Stanley.
Moses. Ah! there is the pity of all: he is so damned charitable.
Rowley. And I left a hosier and two tailors in the hall, who, I'm sure, won't be paid, and this hundred would satisfy them.
Sir Oliver. Well, well, I'll pay his debts, and his benevolence too. But now I am no more a broker, and you shall introduce me to the elder brother as old Stanley.
Rowley. Not yet awhile; Sir Peter, I know, means to call there about this time.

Enter TRIP.

Trip. Oh, gentlemen, I beg pardon for not showing you out; this way—Moses, a word. (*Exit with* MOSES.)
Sir Oliver. There's a fellow for you! Would you believe it, that puppy intercepted the Jew on our coming, and wanted to raise money before he got to his master!
Rowley. Indeed.

Sir Oliver. Yes, they are now planning an annuity business. Ah, Master Rowley, in my days servants were content with the follies of their masters when they were worn a little threadbare; but now they have their vices, like their birthday clothes,³² with the gloss on.   *Exeunt.*

SCENE III: *A Library in* JOSEPH SURFACE'S *House.*

Enter JOSEPH SURFACE *and* SERVANT.

Joseph Surface. No letter from Lady Teazle?
Servant. No, sir.
Joseph Surface. (*Aside.*) I am surprised she has not sent, if she is prevented from coming. Sir Peter certainly does not suspect me. Yet I wish I may not lose the heiress through the scrape I have drawn myself into with the wife. However, Charles's imprudence and bad character are great points in my favour.   (*Knocking.*)
Servant. Sir, I believe that must be Lady Teazle.
Joseph Surface. Hold! See whether it is or not before you go to the door. I have a particular message for you if it should be my brother.
Servant. 'Tis her ladyship, sir; she always leaves the chair at the milliner's in the next street.
Joseph Surface. Stay, stay! Draw that screen before the window—that will do;—my opposite neighbour is a maiden lady of so curious a temper.—(SERVANT *draws the screen, and exit.*) I have a difficult hand to play in this affair. Lady Teazle has lately suspected my views on Maria; but she must by no means be let into that secret—at least, till I have her more in my power.

Enter LADY TEAZLE.

Lady Teazle. What, sentiment in soliloquy now? Have you been very impatient? O lud! don't pretend to look grave. I vow I couldn't come before.
Joseph Surface. O madam, punctuality is a species of constancy very unfashionable in a lady of quality.
Lady Teazle. Upon my word, you ought to pity me. Do you know Sir Peter is grown so illnatured to me of late, and so jealous of Charles too—that's the best of the story, isn't it?
Joseph Surface. (*Aside.*) I am glad my scandalous friends keep that up.
Lady Teazle. I am sure I wish he would let Maria marry

him, and then perhaps he would be convinced; don't you, Mr. Surface?

Joseph Surface. (*Aside.*) Indeed I do not.—(*Aloud.*) Oh, certainly I do! for then my dear Lady Teazle would also be convinced how wrong her suspicions were of my having any design on the silly girl.

Lady Teazle. Well, well, I'm inclined to believe you. But isn't it provoking to have the most illnatured things said at one? And there's my friend Lady Sneerwell has circulated I don't know how many scandalous tales of me, and all without any foundation, too; that's what vexes me.

Joseph Surface. Ay, madam, to be sure, that is the provoking circumstance—without foundation; yes, yes, there's the mortification, indeed; for, when a scandalous story is believed against one, there certainly is no comfort like the consciousness of having deserved it.

Lady Teazle. No, to be sure, then I'd forgive their malice; but to attack me, who am really so innocent, and who never say an illnatured thing of anybody—that is, of any friend; and then Sir Peter, too, to have him so peevish, and so suspicious, when I know the integrity of my own heart—indeed 'tis monstrous!

Joseph Surface. But, my dear Lady Teazle, 'tis your own fault if you suffer it. When a husband entertains a groundless suspicion of his wife, and withdraws his confidence from her, the original compact is broken, and she owes it to the honor of her sex to endeavor to outwit him.

Lady Teazle. Indeed! So that, if he suspects me without cause, it follows, that the best way of curing his jealousy is to give him reason for't?

Joseph Surface. Undoubtedly—for your husband should never be deceived in you: and in that case it becomes you to be frail in compliment to his discernment.

Lady Teazle. To be sure, what you say is very reasonable, and when the consciousness of my innocence——

Joseph Surface. Ah, my dear madam, there is the great mistake; 'tis this very conscious innocence that is of the greatest prejudice to you. What is it makes you negligent of forms, and careless of the world's opinion? why, the consciousness of your own innocence. What makes you thoughtless in your conduct and apt to run into a thousand little imprudences? why, the consciousness of your own innocence. What makes you impatient of Sir Peter's temper, and outrageous at his suspicions? why, the consciousness of your innocence.

Lady Teazle. 'Tis very true!

Joseph Surface. Now, my dear Lady Teazle, if you would

but once make a trifling *faux pas*, you can't conceive how cautious you would grow, and how ready to humor and agree with your husband.

Lady Teazle. Do you think so?

Joseph Surface. Oh, I'm sure on't! and then you would find all scandal would cease at once, for—in short, your character at present is like a person in a plethora, absolutely dying from too much health.

Lady Teazle. So, so; then I perceive your prescription is that I must sin in my own defence, and part with my virtue to preserve my reputation?

Joseph Surface. Exactly so, upon my credit, ma'am.

Lady Teazle. Well, certainly this is the oddest doctrine, and the newest receipt for avoiding calumny?

Joseph Surface. An infallible one, believe me. Prudence, like experience, must be paid for.

Lady Teazle. Why, if my understanding were once convinced——

Joseph Surface. Oh, certainly, madam, your understanding should be convinced. Yes, yes—Heaven forbid I should persuade you to do anything you thought wrong. No, no, I have too much honor to desire it.

Lady Teazle. Don't you think we may as well leave honor out of the argument?   (*Rises.*)

Joseph Surface. Ah, the ill effects of your country education, I see, still remain with you.

Lady Teazle. I doubt they do, indeed; and I will fairly own to you, that if I could be persuaded to do wrong, it would be by Sir Peter's ill usage sooner than your honorable logic, after all.

Joseph Surface. Then, by this hand, which he is unworthy of——   (*Taking her hand.*)

Enter SERVANT.

'Sdeath, you blockhead—what do you want?

Servant. I beg your pardon, sir, but I thought you would not choose Sir Peter to come up without announcing him.

Joseph Surface. Sir Peter!—Oons—the devil!

Lady Teazle. Sir Peter! O lud! I'm ruined! I'm ruined!

Servant. Sir, 'twasn't I let him in.

Lady Teazle. Oh! I'm quite undone! What will become of me now, Mr. Logic?—Oh! mercy, he's on the stairs—I'll get behind here—and if I'm so imprudent again——

(*Goes behind the screen.*)

Joseph Surface. Give me that book.

(*Sits down.* SERVANT *pretends to adjust his chair.*)

Enter Sir Peter Teazle.

Sir Peter. Ay, ever improving himself. Mr. Surface, Mr. Surface——

Joseph Surface. Oh, my dear Sir Peter, I beg your pardon. (*Gaping, throws away the book.*) I have been dozing over a stupid book. Well, I am much obliged to you for this call. You haven't been here, I believe, since I fitted up this room. Books, you know, are the only things I am a coxcomb in.

Sir Peter. 'Tis very neat indeed. Well, well, that's proper; and you can make even your screen a source of knowledge—hung, I perceive, with maps.

Joseph Surface. Oh, yes, I find great use in that screen.

Sir Peter. I dare say you must, certainly, when you want to find anything in a hurry.

Joseph Surface. (*Aside.*) Ay, or to hide anything in a hurry either.

Sir Peter. Well, I have a little private business——

Joseph Surface. (*To* Servant.) You need not stay.

Servant. No, sir.   *Exit.*

Joseph Surface. Here's a chair, Sir Peter—I beg——

Sir Peter. Well, now we are alone, there is a subject, my dear friend, on which I wish to unburden my mind to you—a point of the greatest moment to my peace; in short, my good friend, Lady Teazle's conduct of late has made me very unhappy.

Joseph Surface. Indeed! I am very sorry to hear it.

Sir Peter. Yes, 'tis but too plain she has not the least regard for me; but, what's worse, I have pretty good authority to suppose she has formed an attachment to another.

Joseph Surface. Indeed! you astonish me!

Sir Peter. Yes! and, between ourselves, I think I've discovered the person.

Joseph Surface. How! you alarm me exceedingly.

Sir Peter. Ay, my dear friend, I knew you would sympathize with me!

Joseph Surface. Yes, believe me, Sir Peter, such a discovery would hurt me just as much as it would you.

Sir Peter. I am convinced of it. Ah! it is a happiness to have a friend whom we can trust even with one's family secrets. But have you no guess who I mean?

Joseph Surface. I haven't the most distant idea. It can't be Sir Benjamin Backbite!

Sir Peter. Oh no! what say you to Charles?

Joseph Surface. My brother! impossible!

Sir Peter. Oh, my dear friend, the goodness of your own heart misleads you. You judge of others by yourself.

Joseph Surface. Certainly, Sir Peter, the heart that is conscious of its own integrity is ever slow to credit another's treachery.

Sir Peter. True; but your brother has no sentiment—you never hear him talk so.

Joseph Surface. Yet I can't but think Lady Teazle herself has too much principle.

Sir Peter. Ay; but what is principle against the flattery of a handsome, lively young fellow?

Joseph Surface. That's very true.

Sir Peter. And then, you know, the difference of our ages makes it very improbable that she should have any great affection for me; and if she were to be frail, and I were to make it public, why the town would only laugh at me, the foolish old bachelor who had married a girl.

Joseph Surface. That's true, to be sure—they would laugh.

Sir Peter. Laugh! ay, and make ballads, and paragraphs, and the devil knows what of me.

Joseph Surface. No, you must never make it public.

Sir Peter. But then again—that the nephew of my old friend, Sir Oliver, should be the person to attempt such a wrong, hurts me more nearly.

Joseph Surface. Ay, there's the point. When ingratitude barbs the dart of injury, the wound has double danger in it.

Sir Peter. Ay—I that was, in a manner, left his guardian, in whose house he had been so often entertained, who never in my life denied him—my advice!

Joseph Surface. Oh, 'tis not to be credited! There may be a man capable of such baseness, to be sure; but, for my part, till you can give me positive proofs, I cannot but doubt it. However, if it should be proved on him, he is no longer a brother of mine—I disclaim kindred with him: for the man who can break the laws of hospitality and tempt the wife of his friend, deserves to be branded as the pest of society.

Sir Peter. What a difference there is between you! What noble sentiments!

Joseph Surface. Yet I cannot suspect Lady Teazle's honor.

Sir Peter. I am sure I wish to think well of her, and to remove all ground of quarrel between us. She has lately reproached me more than once with having made no settlement on her; and, in our last quarrel, she almost hinted that she should not break her heart if I was dead. Now, as we seem to differ in our ideas of expense, I have resolved she shall have her own way and be her own mistress in that respect for the future; and, if I were to die, she will find I have not been inattentive to her interest while living. Here, my friend, are the drafts of two deeds, which I wish to have your opinion on. By one, she will enjoy eight hundred a year independent while I live; and, by the other, the bulk of my fortune at my death.

Joseph Surface. This conduct, Sir Peter, is indeed truly generous.—(*Aside.*) I wish it may not corrupt my pupil.

Sir Peter. Yes, I am determined she shall have no cause to complain, though I would not have her acquainted with the latter instance of my affection yet awhile.

Joseph Surface. (*Aside.*) Nor I, if I could help it.

Sir Peter. And now, my dear friend, if you please, we will talk over the situation of your hopes with Maria.

Joseph Surface. (*Softly.*) Oh, no, Sir Peter; another time, if you please.

Sir Peter. I am sensibly chagrined at the little progress you seem to make in her affections.

Joseph Surface. (*Softly.*) I beg you will not mention it. What are my disappointments when your happiness is in debate!—(*Aside.*) 'Sdeath, I shall be ruined every way!

Sir Peter. And though you are averse to my acquainting Lady Teazle with your passion, I'm sure she's not your enemy in the affair.

Joseph Surface. Pray, Sir Peter, now oblige me. I am really too much affected by the subject we have been speaking of to bestow a thought on my own concerns. The man who is entrusted with his friend's distresses can never——

Enter SERVANT.

Well, sir?

Servant. Your brother, sir, is speaking to a gentleman in the street, and says he knows you are within.

Joseph Surface. 'Sdeath, blockhead, I'm not within—I'm out for the day.

Sir Peter. Stay—hold—a thought has struck me: you shall be at home.

Joseph Surface. Well, well, let him up—(*Exit* SERVANT.) (*Aside.*) He'll interrupt Sir Peter, however.

Sir Peter. Now, my good friend, oblige me, I entreat you. Before Charles comes, let me conceal myself somewhere, then do you tax him on the point we have been talking, and his answer may satisfy me at once.

Joseph Surface. Oh, fie, Sir Peter! would you have me join in so mean a trick?—to trepan my brother too?

Sir Peter. Nay, you tell me you are sure he is innocent; if so, you do him the greatest service by giving him an opportunity to clear himself, and you will set my heart at rest. Come, you shall not refuse me: here, behind the screen will be—Hey! what the devil! there seems to be one listener here already—I'll swear I saw a petticoat!

Joseph Surface. Ha! ha! ha! Well, this is ridiculous enough. I'll tell you, Sir Peter, though I hold man of intrigue to be a most despicable character, yet you know, it does not follow that one is to be an absolute Joseph either! Hark'ee, 'tis a little French milliner, a silly rogue that plagues me; and having some character to lose, on your coming, sir, she ran behind the screen.

Sir Peter. Ah, you rogue—— But, egad, she has overheard all I have been saying of my wife.

Joseph Surface. Oh, 'twill never go any farther, you may depend upon it!

Sir Peter. No! then, faith, let her hear it out.—Here's a closet will do as well.

Joseph Surface. Well, go in there.

Sir Peter. Sly rogue! sly rogue!   (*Goes into the closet.*)

Joseph Surface. A narrow escape, indeed! and a curious situation I'm in, to part man and wife in this manner.

Lady Teazle. (*Peeping.*) Couldn't I steal off?

Joseph Surface. Keep close, my angel.

Sir Peter. (*Peeping.*) Joseph, tax me home!

Joseph Surface. Back, my dear friend!

Lady Teazle. (*Peeping.*) Couldn't you lock Sir Peter in?

Joseph Surface. Be still, my life!

Sir Peter. (*Peeping.*) You're sure the little milliner won't blab?

Joseph Surface. In, in, my dear Sir Peter!—'Fore gad, I wish I had a key to the door!

Enter Charles Surface.

Charles Surface. Holla! brother, what has been the matter? Your fellow would not let me up at first. What! have you had a Jew or a wench with you?

Joseph Surface. Neither, brother, I assure you.

Charles Surface. But what has made Sir Peter steal off? I thought he had been with you.

Joseph Surface. He was, brother; but, hearing you were coming, he did not choose to stay.

Charles Surface. What! was the old gentleman afraid I wanted to borrow money of him!

Joseph Surface. No, sir: but I am sorry to find, Charles, you have lately given that worthy man grounds for great uneasiness.

Charles Surface. Yes, they tell me I do that to a great many worthy men. But how so, pray?

Joseph Surface. To be plain with you, brother, he thinks you are endeavoring to gain Lady Teazle's affections from him.

Charles Surface. Who, I? O lud! not I, upon my word.— Ha! ha! ha! ha! so the old fellow has found out that he has got a young wife, has he?—or, what's worse, Lady Teazle has found out she has an old husband?

Joseph Surface. This is no subject to jest on, brother. He who can laugh——

Charles Surface. True, true, as you were going to say— then, seriously, I never had the least idea of what you charge me with, upon my honor.

Joseph Surface. (*In a loud voice.*) Well, it will give Sir Peter great satisfaction to hear this.

Charles Surface. To be sure, I once thought the lady seemed to have taken a fancy to me; but, upon my soul, I never gave her the least encouragement. Besides, you know my attachment to Maria.

Joseph Surface. But sure, brother, even if Lady Teazle had betrayed the fondest partiality for you——

Charles Surface. Why, look'ee, Joseph, I hope I shall never deliberately do a dishonorable action; but if a pretty woman was purposely to throw herself in my way—and that pretty woman married to a man old enough to be her father——

Joseph Surface. Well!

Charles Surface. Why, I believe I should be obliged to borrow a little of your morality, that's all. But, brother, do you know now that you surprise me exceedingly by naming me with Lady Teazle; for i'faith, I always understood you were her favorite.

Joseph Surface. Oh, for shame, Charles! This retort is foolish.

Charles Surface. Nay, I swear I have seen you exchange such significant glances——

Joseph Surface. Nay, nay, sir, this is no jest.

Charles Surface. Egad, I'm serious! Don't you remember one day when I called here——

Joseph Surface. Nay, prithee, Charles——

Charles Surface. And found you together——

Joseph Surface. Zounds, sir, I insist——

Charles Surface. And another time, when your servant——

Joseph Surface. Brother, brother, a word with you! (*Aside.*) Gad, I must stop him.

Charles Surface. Informed, I say, that——

Joseph Surface. Hush! I beg your pardon, but Sir Peter

has overheard all we have been saying. I knew you would clear yourself, or I should not have consented.

Charles Surface. How, Sir Peter! Where is he?

Joseph Surface. Softly, there!   (*Points to the closet.*)

Charles Surface. Oh, 'fore Heaven, I'll have him out. Sir Peter, come forth!

Joseph Surface. No, no——

Charles Surface. I say, Sir Peter, come into court.—(*Pulls in* SIR PETER.) What! my old guardian!—What!—turn inquisitor and take evidence incog.?

Sir Peter. Give me your hand, Charles—I believe I have suspected you wrongfully; but you mustn't be angry with Joseph—'twas my plan!

Charles Surface. Indeed!

Sir Peter. But I acquit you. I promise you I don't think near so ill of you as I did. What I have heard has given me great satisfaction.

Charles Surface. Egad, then, 'twas lucky you didn't hear any more. Wasn't it, Joseph?

Sir Peter. Ah! you would have retorted on him.

Charles Surface. Ah, ay, that was a joke.

Sir Peter. Yes, yes, I know his honor too well.

Charles Surface. But you might as well have suspected him as me in this matter, for all that. Mightn't he, Joseph?

Sir Peter. Well, well, I believe you.

Joseph Surface. (*Aside.*) Would they were both out of the room!

Sir Peter. And in future, perhaps, we may not be such strangers.

Enter SERVANT *and whispers* JOSEPH SURFACE.

Joseph Surface. Gentlemen, I beg pardon—I must wait on you downstairs; here's a person come on particular business.

Charles Surface. Well, you can see him in another room. Sir Peter and I have not met a long time, and I have something to say to him.

Joseph Surface. (*Aside.*) They must not be left together.—(*Aloud.*) I'll send Lady Sneerwell away, and return directly.—(*Aside to* SIR PETER.) Sir Peter, not a word of the French milliner.

Sir Peter. (*Aside to* JOSEPH SURFACE.) I! not for the world!—(*Exit* JOSEPH SURFACE.) Ah, Charles, if you associated more with your brother, one might indeed hope for your reformation. He is a man of sentiment. Well, there is nothing in the world so noble as a man of sentiment.

Charles Surface. Psha! he is too moral by half; and so apprehensive of his good name, as he calls it, that I suppose he would as soon let a priest into his house as a wench.

Sir Peter. No, no,—come, come,—you wrong him. No, no, Joseph is no rake, but he is no such saint either, in that respect.—(*Aside.*) I have a great mind to tell him—we should have such a laugh at Joseph.

Charles Surface. Oh, hang him! he's a very anchorite, a young hermit!

Sir Peter. Hark'ee—you must not abuse him: he may chance to hear of it again, I promise you.

Charles Surface. Why, you won't tell him?

Sir Peter. No—but—this way.—(*Aside.*) Egad, I'll tell him. (*Aloud.*) Hark'ee, have you a mind to have a good laugh at Joseph?

Charles Surface. I should like it of all things.

Sir Peter. Then, i'faith, we will! I'll be quit with him for discovering me. He had a girl with him when I called.

Charles Surface. What! Joseph? you jest.

Sir Peter. Hush!—a little French milliner—and the best of the jest is—she's in the room now.

Charles Surface. The devil she is!

Sir Peter. Hush! I tell you. (*Points to the screen.*)

Charles Surface. Behind the screen! S'life, let's unveil her!

Sir Peter. No, no, he's coming. You shan't indeed!

Charles Surface. Oh, egad, we'll have a peep at the little milliner!

Sir Peter. Not for the world!—Joseph will never forgive me.

Charles Surface. I'll stand by you——

Sir Peter. Odds, here he is!

JOSEPH SURFACE *enters just as* CHARLES *throws down the screen.*

Charles Surface. Lady Teazle, by all that's wonderful!

Sir Peter. Lady Teazle, by all that's damnable!

Charles Surface. Sir Peter, this is one of the smartest French milliners I ever saw. Egad, you seem all to have been diverting yourselves here at hide and seek, and I don't see who is out of the secret. Shall I beg your ladyship to inform me? Not a word!—Brother, will you be pleased to explain this matter? What! is Morality dumb too?—Sir Peter, though I found you in the dark, perhaps you are not so now! All mute! Well—though I can make nothing of the affair, I suppose you perfectly understand one another; so I'll leave you to yourselves. (*Going.*) Brother, I'm sorry to find you have given that worthy man grounds for so much uneasiness.— Sir Peter! there's nothing in the world so noble as a man of sentiment!   *Exit.*

They stand for some time looking at each other.

Joseph Surface. Sir Peter—notwithstanding—I confess— that appearances are against me—if you will afford me your patience—I make no doubt—but I shall explain everything to your satisfaction.

Sir Peter. If you please, sir.

Joseph Surface. The fact is, sir, that Lady Teazle, know- ing my pretensions to your ward Maria—I say, sir, Lady Teazle, being apprehensive of the jealousy of your temper— and knowing my friendship to the family—she, sir, I say— called here—in order that—I might explain these pretensions —but on your coming—being apprehensive—as I said—of your jealousy—she withdrew—and this, you may depend on it, is the whole truth of the matter.

Sir Peter. A very clear account, upon my word; and I dare swear the lady will vouch for every article of it.

Lady Teazle. For not one word of it, Sir Peter!

Sir Peter. How! don't you think it worth while to agree in the lie?

Lady Teazle. There is not one syllable of truth in what that gentleman has told you.

Sir Peter. I believe you, upon my soul, ma'am!

Joseph Surface. (*Aside to* LADY TEAZLE.) S'death, madam, will you betray me?

Lady Teazle. Good Mr. Hypocrite, by your leave, I'll speak for myself.

Sir Peter. Ay, let her alone, sir; you'll find she'll make out a better story than you, without prompting.

Lady Teazle. Hear me, Sir Peter! I came here on no mat- ter relating to your ward, and even ignorant of this gentle- man's pretensions to her. But I came, seduced by his in- sidious arguments, at least to listen to his pretended passion, if not to sacrifice your honor to his baseness.

Sir Peter. Now, I believe, the truth is coming, indeed!

Joseph Surface. The woman's mad!

Lady Teazle. No, sir; she has recovered her senses, and your own arts have furnished her with the means. Sir Peter, I do not expect you to credit me—but the tenderness you expressed for me, when I am sure you could not think I was a witness to it, has penetrated so to my heart, that had I left the place without the shame of this discovery, my future life should have spoken the sincerity of my gratitude. As for that smooth-tongued hypocrite, who would have seduced the wife of his too credulous friend, while he affected honorable addresses to his ward—I behold him now in a light so truly despicable that I shall never again respect myself for having listened to him.   *Exit.*

Joseph Surface. Notwithstanding all this, Sir Peter, Heaven knows——

Sir Peter. That you are a villain! and so I leave you to your conscience.

Joseph Surface. You are too rash, Sir Peter; you shall hear me. The man who shuts out conviction by refusing to——

Exeunt, JOSEPH SURFACE *talking.*

ACT V

SCENE I: *The Library in* JOSEPH SURFACE'S *House.*

Enter JOSEPH SURFACE *and* SERVANT.

Joseph Surface. Mr. Stanley! and why should you think I would see him? you must know he comes to ask something.

Servant. Sir, I should not have let him in, but that Mr. Rowley came to the door with him.

Joseph Surface. Psha! blockhead! to suppose that I should now be in a temper to receive visits from poor relations!— Well, why don't you show the fellow up?

Servant. I will, sir.—Why, sir, it was not my fault that Sir Peter discovered my lady——

Joseph Surface. Go, fool!—(*Exit* SERVANT.) Sure fortune never played a man of my policy such a trick before! My character with Sir Peter, my hopes with Maria, destroyed in a moment! I'm in a rare humor to listen to other people's distresses! I shan't be able to bestow even a benevolent senti-ment on Stanley—So! here he comes, and Rowley with him. I must try to recover myself, and put a little charity in my face, however.   *Exit.*

Enter SIR OLIVER SURFACE *and* ROWLEY.

Sir Oliver. What! does he avoid us? That was he, was it not?

Rowley. It was, sir. But I doubt you are coming a little too abruptly. His nerves are so weak that the sight of a poor relation may be too much for him. I should have gone first to break it to him.

Sir Oliver. Oh, plague of his nerves! Yet this is he whom Sir Peter extols as a man of the most benevolent way of thinking!

Rowley. As to his way of thinking, I cannot pretend to decide; for, to do him justice, he appears to have as much speculative benevolence as any private gentleman in the kingdom, though he is seldom so sensual as to indulge himself in the exercise of it.

Sir Oliver. Yet he has a string of charitable sentiments at his fingers' ends.

Rowley. Or, rather, at his tongue's end, Sir Oliver; for I believe there is no sentiment he has such faith in as that "Charity begins at home."

Sir Oliver. And his, I presume, is of that domestic sort which never stirs abroad at all.

Rowley. I doubt you'll find it so;—but he's coming. I mustn't seem to interrupt you; and you know, immediately as you leave him, I come in to announce your arrival in your real character.

Sir Oliver. True; and afterwards you'll meet me at Sir Peter's.

Rowley. Without losing a moment.   *Exit.*

Sir Oliver. I don't like the complaisance of his features.

Enter JOSEPH SURFACE.

Joseph Surface. Sir, I beg you ten thousand pardons for keeping you a moment waiting.—Mr. Stanley, I presume.

Sir Oliver. At your service.

Joseph Surface. Sir, I beg you will do me the honor to sit down—I entreat you, sir.

Sir Oliver. Dear sir—there's no occasion.—(*Aside.*) Too civil by half!

Joseph Surface. I have not the pleasure of knowing you, Mr. Stanley; but I am extremely happy to see you look so well. You were nearly related to my mother, I think, Mr. Stanley?

Sir Oliver. I was, sir; so nearly that my present poverty, I fear, may do discredit to her wealthy children, else I should not have presumed to trouble you.

Joseph Surface. Dear sir, there needs no apology: he that is in distress, though a stranger, has a right to claim kindred with the wealthy. I am sure I wish I was one of that class, and had it in my power to offer you even a small relief.

Sir Oliver. If your uncle, Sir Oliver, were here, I should have a friend.

Joseph Surface. I wish he was, sir, with all my heart: you should not want an advocate with him, believe me, sir.

Sir Oliver. I should not need one—my distresses would recommend me. But I imagined his bounty would enable you to become the agent of his charity.

Joseph Surface. My dear sir, you were strangely misinformed. Sir Oliver is a worthy man, a very worthy man, but avarice, Mr. Stanley, is the vice of age. I will tell you, my good sir, in confidence, what he has done for me has been a mere nothing; though people, I know, have thought otherwise; and, for my part, I never choose to contradict the report.

Sir Oliver. What! has he never transmitted you bullion—rupees—pagodas? [33]

Joseph Surface. Oh, dear sir, nothing of the kind! No, no; a few presents now and then—china, shawls, congou tea,[34] avadavats,[35] and Indian crackers [36]—little more, believe me.

Sir Oliver. (*Aside.*) Here's gratitude for twelve thousand pounds!—Avadavats and Indian crackers!

Joseph Surface. Then, my dear sir, you have heard, I doubt not, of the extravagance of my brother; there are very few would credit what I have done for that unfortunate young man.

Sir Oliver. (*Aside.*) Not I, for one!

Joseph Surface. The sums I have lent him! Indeed I have been exceedingly to blame; it was an amiable weakness; however, I don't pretend to defend it—and now I feel it doubly culpable, since it has deprived me of the pleasure of serving you, Mr. Stanley, as my heart dictates.

Sir Oliver. (*Aside.*) Dissembler!—(*Aloud.*) Then, sir, you can't assist me?

Joseph Surface. At present, it grieves me to say, I cannot; but, whenever I have the ability, you may depend upon hearing from me.

Sir Oliver. I am extremely sorry——

Joseph Surface. Not more than I, believe me; to pity, without the power to relieve, is still more painful than to ask and be denied.

Sir Oliver. Kind sir, your most obedient humble servant.

Joseph Surface. You leave me deeply affected, Mr. Stanley.—William, be ready to open the door.

Sir Oliver. Oh, dear sir, no ceremony.

Joseph Surface. Your very obedient.

Sir Oliver. Sir, your most obsequious.

Joseph Surface. You may depend upon hearing from me, whenever I can be of service.

Sir Oliver. Sweet sir, you are too good.

Joseph Surface. In the meantime I wish you health and spirits.

Sir Oliver. Your ever grateful and perpetual humble servant.

Joseph Surface. Sir, yours as sincerely.

Sir Oliver. (*Aside.*) Charles!—you are my heir.   *Exit.*

Joseph Surface. This is one bad effect of a good character; it invites application from the unfortunate, and there needs no small degree of address to gain the reputation of benevolence without incurring the expense. The silver ore of pure charity is an expensive article in the catalogue of a man's good qualities; whereas the sentimental French plate I use instead of it makes just as good a show, and pays no tax.

Enter ROWLEY.

Rowley. Mr. Surface, your servant: I was apprehensive of interrupting you, though my business demands immediate attention, as this note will inform you.

Joseph Surface. Always happy to see Mr. Rowley.— (*Reads.*) Sir Oliver Surface!—My uncle arrived!

Rowley. He is, indeed: we have just parted—quite well, after a speedy voyage, and impatient to embrace his worthy nephew.

Joseph Surface. I am astonished!—William! stop Mr. Stanley, if he's not gone.

Rowley. Oh! he's out of reach, I believe.

Joseph Surface. Why did you not let me know this when you came in together?

Rowley. I thought you had particular business. But I must be gone to inform your brother and appoint him here to meet your uncle. He will be with you in a quarter of an hour.

Joseph Surface. So he says. Well, I am strangely overjoyed at his coming.—(*Aside.*) Never, to be sure, was anything so damned unlucky!

Rowley. You will be delighted to see how well he looks.

Joseph Surface. Oh! I'm overjoyed to hear it.—(*Aside.*) —Just at this time!

Rowley. I'll tell him how impatiently you expect him.

Joseph Surface. Do, do; pray give my best duty and affection. Indeed, I cannot express the sensations I feel at the thought of seeing him.—(*Exit* ROWLEY.) Certainly his coming just at this time is the cruellest piece of ill fortune. *Exit.*

SCENE II: SIR PETER TEAZLE'S *House.*

Enter MRS. CANDOUR *and* MAID.

Maid. Indeed, ma'am, my lady will see nobody at present.

Mrs. Candour. Did you tell her it was her friend Mrs. Candour?

Maid. Yes, ma'am; but she begs you will excuse her.

Mrs. Candour. Do go again; I shall be glad to see her, if it be only for a moment, for I am sure she must be in great distress.—(*Exit* MAID.) Dear heart, how provoking! I'm not mistress of half the circumstances! We shall have the whole affair in the newspapers, with the names of the parties at length, before I have dropped the story at a dozen houses.

Enter SIR BENJAMIN BACKBITE.

Oh, dear Sir Benjamin! you have heard, I suppose——

Sir Benjamin. Of Lady Teazle and Mr. Surface——

Mrs. Candour. And Sir Peter's discovery——

Sir Benjamin. Oh, the strangest piece of business, to be sure!

Mrs. Candour. Well, I never was so surprised in my life. I am so sorry for all parties, indeed.

Sir Benjamin. Now, I don't pity Sir Peter at all: he was so extravagantly partial to Mr. Surface.

Mrs. Candour. Mr. Surface! Why, 'twas with Charles Lady Teazle was detected.

Sir Benjamin. No, no, I tell you: Mr. Surface is the gallant.

Mrs. Candour. No such thing! Charles is the man. 'Twas Mr. Surface brought Sir Peter on purpose to discover them.

Sir Benjamin. I tell you I had it from one——

Mrs. Candour. And I have it from one——

Sir Benjamin. Who had it from one, who had it——

Mrs. Candour. From one immediately——But here comes Lady Sneerwell; perhaps she knows the whole affair.

Enter LADY SNEERWELL.

Lady Sneerwell. So, my dear Mrs. Candour, here's a sad affair of our friend Lady Teazle!

Mrs. Candour. Ay, my dear friend, who would have thought——

Lady Sneerwell. Well, there is no trusting to appearances; though indeed, she was always too lively for me.

Mrs. Candour. To be sure, her manners were a little too free; but then she was so young!

Lady Sneerwell. And had, indeed, some good qualities.

Mrs. Candour. So she had, indeed. But have you heard the particulars?

Lady Sneerwell. No; but everybody says that Mr. Surface——

Sir Benjamin. Ay, there; I told you Mr. Surface was the man.

Mrs. Candour. No, no: indeed the assignation was with Charles.

Lady Sneerwell. With Charles! You alarm me, Mrs. Candour.

Mrs. Candour. Yes, yes: he was the lover. Mr. Surface, to do him justice, was only the informer.

Sir Benjamin. Well, I'll not dispute with you, Mrs. Candour; but, be it which it may, I hope that Sir Peter's wound will not——

Mrs. Candour. Sir Peter's wound! Oh, mercy! I didn't hear a word of their fighting.

Lady Sneerwell. Nor I, a syllable.

Sir Benjamin. No! what, no mention of the duel?

Mrs. Candour. Not a word.

Sir Benjamin. Oh, yes: they fought before they left the room.

Lady Sneerwell. Pray let us hear.

Mrs. Candour. Ay, do oblige us with the duel.

Sir Benjamin. "Sir," says Sir Peter, immediately after the discovery, "you are a most ungrateful fellow."

Mrs. Candour. Ay, to Charles——

Sir Benjamin. No, no—to Mr. Surface—"a most ungrateful fellow; and old as I am, sir," says he, "I insist on immediate satisfaction."

Mrs. Candour. Ay, that must have been to Charles; for 'tis very unlikely Mr. Surface should fight in his own house.

Sir Benjamin. 'Gad's life, ma'am, not at all—"giving me immediate satisfaction."—On this, ma'am, Lady Teazle, seeing Sir Peter in such danger, ran out of the room in strong hysterics, and Charles after her, calling out for hartshorn and water; then, madam, they began to fight with swords——

Enter CRABTREE.

Crabtree. With pistols, nephew—pistols! I have it from undoubted authority.

Mrs. Candour. Oh, Mr. Crabtree, then it is all true!

Crabtree. Too true, indeed, madam, and Sir Peter is dangerously wounded——

Sir Benjamin. By a thrust in *seconde* [37] quite through his left side——

Crabtree. By a bullet lodged in the thorax.

Mrs. Candour. Mercy on me! Poor Sir Peter!

Crabtree. Yes, madam; though Charles would have avoided the matter, if he could.

Mrs. Candour. I knew Charles was the person.

Sir Benjamin. My uncle, I see, knows nothing of the matter.

Crabtree. But Sir Peter taxed him with the basest ingratitude——

Sir Benjamin. That I told you, you know——

Crabtree. Do, nephew, let me speak!—and insisted on immediate——

Sir Benjamin. Just as I said——

Crabtree. Odds life, nephew, allow others to know something too! A pair of pistols lay on the bureau (for Mr. Surface, it seems, had come home the night before late from Salthill where he had been to see the Montem [38] with a friend who has a son at Eton) so, unluckily, the pistols were left charged.

Sir Benjamin. I heard nothing of this.

Crabtree. Sir Peter forced Charles to take one, and they fired, it seems, pretty nearly together. Charles's shot took effect, as I tell you, and Sir Peter's missed; but, what is very extraordinary, the ball struck against a little bronze Shakespeare that stood over the fireplace, grazed out of the window at a right angle, and wounded the postman who was just coming to the door with a double letter [39] from Northamptonshire.

Sir Benjamin. My uncle's account is more circumstantial, I confess; but I believe mine is the true one for all that.

Lady Sneerwell. (*Aside.*) I am more interested in this affair than they imagine, and must have better information.

Exit.

Sir Benjamin. Ah! Lady Sneerwell's alarm is very easily accounted for.

Crabtree. Yes, yes, they certainly do say—but that's neither here nor there.

Mrs. Candour. But, pray, where is Sir Peter at present?

Crabtree. Oh! they brought him home, and he is now in the house, though the servants are ordered to deny him.

Mrs. Candour. I believe so, and Lady Teazle, I suppose, attending him.

Crabtree. Yes, yes; and I saw one of the faculty [40] enter just before me.

Sir Benjamin. Hey! who comes here?

Crabtree. Oh, this is he: the physician, depend on't.

Mrs. Candour. Oh, certainly! it must be the physician; and now we shall know.

Enter SIR OLIVER SURFACE.

Crabtree. Well, doctor, what hopes?

Mrs. Candour. Ay, doctor, how's your patient?

Sir Benjamin. Now, doctor, isn't it a wound with a small-sword?

Crabtree. A bullet lodged in the thorax, for a hundred!

Sir Oliver. Doctor! a wound with a smallsword! and a bullet in the thorax?—Oons! are you mad, good people?

Sir Benjamin. Perhaps, sir, you are not a doctor?

Sir Oliver. Truly, I am to thank you for my degree, if I am.

Crabtree. Only a friend of Sir Peter's, then, I presume. But, sir, you must have heard of his accident?

Sir Oliver. Not a word!

Crabtree. Not of his being dangerously wounded?

Sir Oliver. The devil he is!

Sir Benjamin. Run through the body——

Crabtree. Shot in the breast——

Sir Benjamin. By one Mr. Surface——

Crabtree. Ay, the younger.

Sir Oliver. Hey! what the plague! you seem to differ strangely in your accounts: however, you agree that Sir Peter is dangerously wounded.

Sir Benjamin. Oh, yes, we agree there.

Crabtree. Yes, yes, I believe there can be no doubt in that.

Sir Oliver. Then, upon my word, for a person in that situation, he is the most imprudent man alive; for here he comes, walking as if nothing at all was the matter.

Enter SIR PETER TEAZLE.

Odds heart, Sir Peter! you are come in good time, I promise you; for we had just given you over!

Sir Benjamin. (*Aside to* CRABTREE.) Egad, uncle, this is the most sudden recovery!

Sir Oliver. Why, man! what do you do out of bed with a smallsword through your body and a bullet lodged in your thorax?

Sir Peter. A smallsword and a bullet?

Sir Oliver. Ay; these gentlemen would have killed you without law or physic, and wanted to dub me a doctor, to make me an accomplice.

Sir Peter. Why, what is all this?

Sir Benjamin. We rejoice, Sir Peter, that the story of the duel is not true and are sincerely sorry for your other misfortune.

Sir Peter. (*Aside.*) So, so; all over the town already.

Crabtree. Though, Sir Peter, you were certainly vastly to blame to marry at your years.

Mrs. Candour. Though, indeed, as Sir Peter made so good a husband, he's very much to be pitied.

Sir Peter. Plague on your pity, ma'am! I desire none of it.

Sir Benjamin. However, Sir Peter, you must not mind the laughing and jests you will meet with on the occasion.

Sir Peter. Sir, sir! I desire to be master in my own house.

Crabtree. 'Tis no uncommon case, that's one comfort.

Sir Peter. I insist on being left to myself. Without ceremony, I insist on your leaving my house directly!

Mrs. Candour. Well, well, we are going; and depend on't, we'll make the best report of it we can. *Exit.*

Sir Peter. Leave my house!

Crabtree. And tell how hardly you've been treated! *Exit.*

Sir Peter. Leave my house!

Sir Benjamin. And how patiently you bear it. *Exit.*

Sir Peter. Fiends! vipers! furies! Oh! that their own venom would choke them!

Sir Oliver. They are very provoking indeed, Sir Peter.

Enter ROWLEY.

Rowley. I heard high words: what has ruffled you, sir?

Sir Peter. Psha! what signifies asking? Do I ever pass a day without my vexations?

Rowley. Well, I'm not inquisitive.

Sir Oliver. Well, Sir Peter, I have seen both my nephews in the manner we proposed.

Sir Peter. A precious couple they are!

Rowley. Yes, and Sir Oliver is convinced that your judgment was right, Sir Peter.

Sir Oliver. Yes, I find Joseph is indeed the man, after all.

Rowley. Ay, as Sir Peter says, he is a man of sentiment.

Sir Oliver. And acts up to the sentiments he professes.

Rowley. It certainly is edification to hear him talk.

Sir Oliver. Oh, he's a model for the young men of the age! But how's this, Sir Peter? you don't join us in your friend Joseph's praise, as I expected.

Sir Peter. Sir Oliver, we live in a damned wicked world, and the fewer we praise the better.

Rowley. What! do you say so, Sir Peter, who were never mistaken in your life?

Sir Peter. Psha! plague on you both! I see by your sneering you have heard the whole affair. I shall go mad among you!

Rowley. Then, to fret you no longer, Sir Peter, we are indeed acquainted with it all. I met Lady Teazle coming from Mr. Surface's so humbled, that she deigned to request me to be her advocate with you.

Sir Peter. And does Sir Oliver know all this?

Sir Oliver. Every circumstance.

Sir Peter. What, of the closet and the screen, hey?

Sir Oliver. Yes, yes, and the little French milliner. Oh, I have been vastly diverted with the story! ha! ha! ha!

Sir Peter. 'Twas very pleasant.

Sir Oliver. I never laughed more in my life, I assure you: ha! ha! ha!

Sir Peter. Oh, vastly diverting! ha! ha! ha!

Rowley. To be sure, Joseph with his sentiments! ha! ha! ha!

Sir Peter. Yes, yes, his sentiments! ha! ha! ha! Hypocritical villain!

Sir Oliver. Ay, and that rogue Charles to pull Sir Peter out of the closet: ha! ha! ha!

Sir Peter. Ha! ha! 'twas devilish entertaining, to be sure!

Sir Oliver. Ha! ha! ha! Egad, Sir Peter, I should like to have seen your face when the screen was thrown down: ha! ha!

Sir Peter. Yes, yes, my face when the screen was thrown down: ha! ha! ha! Oh, I must never show my head again!

Sir Oliver. But come, come, it isn't fair to laugh at you neither, my old friend; though, upon my soul, I can't help it.

Sir Peter. Oh, pray don't restrain your mirth on my account: it does not hurt me at all! I laugh at the whole affair myself. Yes, yes, I think being a standing jest for all one's acquaintance a very happy situation. Oh, yes, and then of a morning to read the paragraphs about Mr. S——, Lady T——, and Sir P——, will be so entertaining!

Rowley. Without affectation, Sir Peter, you may despise the ridicule of fools. But I see Lady Teazle going towards the next room, I am sure you must desire a reconciliation as earnestly as she does.

Sir Oliver. Perhaps my being here prevents her coming to you. Well, I'll leave honest Rowley to mediate between you; but he must bring you all presently to Mr. Surface's where I am now returning, if not to reclaim a libertine, at least to expose hypocrisy.

Sir Peter. Ah, I'll be present at your discovering yourself there with all my heart; though 'tis a vile unlucky place for discoveries.

Rowley. We'll follow.   *Exit* SIR OLIVER.

Sir Peter. She is not coming here, you see, Rowley.

Rowley. No, but she has left the door of that room open, you perceive. See, she is in tears.

Sir Peter. Certainly a little mortification appears very becoming in a wife. Don't you think it will do her good to let her pine a little?

Rowley. Oh, this is ungenerous in you!

Sir Peter. Well, I know not what to think. You remember the letter I found of hers evidently intended for Charles!

Rowley. A mere forgery, Sir Peter! laid in your way on purpose. This is one of the points which I intend Snake shall give you conviction of.

Sir Peter. I wish I were once satisfied of that. She looks this way. What a remarkably elegant turn of the head she has! Rowley, I'll go to her.

Rowley. Certainly.

Sir Peter. Though, when it is known that we are reconciled, people will laugh at me ten times more.

Rowley. Let them laugh, and retort their malice only by showing them you are happy in spite of it.

Sir Peter. I'faith, so I will! and, if I'm not mistaken, we may yet be the happiest couple in the country.

Rowley. Nay, Sir Peter, he who once lays aside suspicion——

Sir Peter. Hold, Master Rowley! if you have any regard for me, never let me hear you utter anything like a sentiment. I have had enough of them to serve me the rest of my life.

Exeunt.

SCENE III: *The Library in* JOSEPH SURFACE'S *House.*

Enter JOSEPH SURFACE *and* LADY SNEERWELL.

Lady Sneerwell. Impossible! Will not Sir Peter immediately be reconciled to Charles, and of course no longer oppose his union with Maria? The thought is distraction to me.

Joseph Surface. Can passion furnish a remedy?

Lady Sneerwell. No, nor cunning either. Oh, I was a fool, an idiot, to league with such a blunderer!

Joseph Surface. Sure, Lady Sneerwell, I am the greatest sufferer; yet you see I bear the accident with calmness.

Lady Sneerwell. Because the disappointment doesn't reach your heart; your interest only attached you to Maria. Had you felt for her what I have for that ungrateful libertine, neither your temper nor hypocrisy could prevent your showing the sharpness of your vexation.

Joseph Surface. But why should your reproaches fall on me for this disappointment?

Lady Sneerwell. Are you not the cause of it? Had you not a sufficient field for your roguery in imposing upon Sir Peter, and supplanting your brother, but you must endeavor to seduce his wife? I hate such an avarice of crimes; 'tis an unfair monopoly, and never prospers.

Joseph Surface. Well, I admit I have been to blame. I confess I deviated from the direct road of wrong, but I don't think we're so totally defeated neither.

Lady Sneerwell. No?

Joseph Surface. You tell me you have made a trial of Snake since we met, and that you still believe him faithful to us?

Lady Sneerwell. I do believe so.

Joseph Surface. And that he has undertaken, should it be necessary, to swear and prove that Charles is at this time contracted by vows and honor to your ladyship, which some of his former letters to you will serve to support?

Lady Sneerwell. This, indeed, might have assisted.

Joseph Surface. Come, come; it is not too late yet. (*Knocking at the door.*) But hark! this is probably my uncle, Sir Oliver: retire to that room; we'll consult further when he's gone.

Lady Sneerwell. Well, but if he should find you out too.

Joseph Surface. Oh, I have no fear of that. Sir Peter will hold his tongue for his own credit's sake—and you may depend on it I shall soon discover Sir Oliver's weak side!

Lady Sneerwell. I have no diffidence [41] of your abilities! only be constant to one roguery at a time.   *Exit.*

Joseph Surface. I will, I will! So! 'tis confounded hard, after such bad fortune, to be baited by one's confederate in evil. Well, at all events, my character is so much better than Charles's that I certainly—hey!—what—this is not Sir Oliver, but old Stanley again. Plague on't that he should return to tease me just now! I shall have Sir Oliver come and find him here—and—

Enter SIR OLIVER SURFACE.

Gad's life, Mr. Stanley, why have you come back to plague me at this time? You must not stay now, upon my word.

Sir Oliver. Sir, I hear your uncle Oliver is expected here, and though he has been so penurious to you, I'll try what he'll do for me.

Joseph Surface. Sir, 'tis impossible for you to stay now, so I must beg——Come any other time, and I promise you, you shall be assisted.

Sir Oliver. No: Sir Oliver and I must be acquainted.

Joseph Surface. Zounds, sir! then I insist on your quitting the room directly.

Sir Oliver. Nay, sir——

Joseph Surface. Sir, I insist on't!—Here, William! show this gentleman out. Since you compel me, sir, not one moment— this is such insolence!   (*Going to push him out.*)

Enter CHARLES SURFACE.

Charles Surface. Heyday! what's the matter now! What the devil have you got hold of my little broker here? Zounds, brother, don't hurt little Premium. What's the matter, my little fellow?

Joseph Surface. So! he has been with you, too, has he?

Charles Surface. To be sure he has. Why, he's as honest a little——But sure, Joseph, you have not been borrowing money too, have you?

Joseph Surface. Borrowing! no! But, brother, you know we expect Sir Oliver here every——

Charles Surface. O gad, that's true! Noll mustn't find the little broker here, to be sure.

Joseph Surface. Yes, Mr. Stanley insists——

Charles Surface. Stanley! why his name's Premium.

Joseph Surface. No, sir, Stanley.

Charles Surface. No, no, Premium.

Joseph Surface. Well, no matter which—but——

Charles Surface. Ay, ay, Stanley or Premium, 'tis the same thing, as you say; for I suppose he goes by half a hundred names, besides A. B. at the coffee-house.[42]   (*Knocking.*)

Joseph Surface. 'Sdeath! here's Sir Oliver at the door. Now I beg, Mr. Stanley——

Charles Surface. Ay, ay, and I beg, Mr. Premium——

Sir Oliver. Gentlemen——

Joseph Surface. Sir, by heaven you shall go!

Charles Surface. Ay, out with him, certainly!

Sir Oliver. This violence——

Joseph Surface. Sir, 'tis your own fault.

Charles Surface. Out with him, to be sure!

(*Both forcing* SIR OLIVER *out.*)

Enter SIR PETER *and* LADY TEAZLE, MARIA, *and* ROWLEY.

Sir Peter. My old friend, Sir Oliver—hey! What in the name of wonder!—here are dutiful nephews—assault their uncle at first visit!

Lady Teazle. Indeed, Sir Oliver, 'twas well we came in to rescue you.

Rowley. Truly it was; for I perceive, Sir Oliver, the character of old Stanley was no protection to you.

Sir Oliver. Nor of Premium either: the necessities of the

former could not extort a shilling from that benevolent gentleman; and now, egad, I stood a chance of faring worse than my ancestors and being knocked down without being bid for.

Joseph Surface. Charles!

Charles Surface. Joseph!

Joseph Surface. 'Tis now complete!

Charles Surface. Very!

Sir Oliver. Sir Peter, my friend, and Rowley too—look on that elder nephew of mine. You know what he has already received from my bounty; and you also know how gladly I would have regarded half my fortune as held in trust for him? judge, then, my disappointment in discovering him to be destitute of truth, charity, and gratitude!

Sir Peter. Sir Oliver, I should be more surprised at this declaration, if I had not myself found him to be mean, treacherous, and hypocritical.

Lady Teazle. And if the gentleman pleads not guilty to these, pray let him call me to his character.

Sir Peter. Then, I believe, we need add no more: if he knows himself, he will consider it as the most perfect punishment that he is known to the world.

Charles Surface. (*Aside.*) If they talk this way to Honesty, what will they say to me, by-and-by?

Sir Oliver. As for that prodigal, his brother, there——

Charles Surface. (*Aside.*) Ay, now comes my turn: the damned family pictures will ruin me!

Joseph Surface. Sir Oliver—uncle, will you honor me with a hearing?

Charles Surface. (*Aside.*) Now, if Joseph would make one of his long speeches, I might recollect myself a little.

Sir Oliver. (*To* JOSEPH.) I suppose you would undertake to justify yourself entirely?

Joseph Surface. I trust I could.

Sir Oliver. (*To* CHARLES.) Well, sir!—and you could justify yourself too, I suppose?

Charles Surface. Not that I know of, Sir Oliver.

Sir Oliver. What!—Little Premium has been let too much into the secret, I suppose?

Charles Surface. True, sir; but they were family secrets, and should not be mentioned again, you know.

Rowley. Come, Sir Oliver, I know you cannot speak of Charles's follies with anger.

Sir Oliver. Odd's heart, no more I can; nor with gravity either. Sir Peter, do you know the rogue bargained with me for all his ancestors; sold me judges and generals by the foot, and maiden aunts as cheap as broken china.

Charles Surface. To be sure, Sir Oliver, I did make a little free with the family canvas, that's the truth on't. My ancestors may rise in judgment against me, there's no denying it; but believe me sincere when I tell you—and upon my soul I would not say so if I was not—that if I do not appear mortified at the exposure of my follies, it is because I feel at this moment the warmest satisfaction at seeing you, my liberal benefactor.

Sir Oliver. Charles, I believe you. Give me your hand again: the ill looking little fellow over the settee has made your peace.

Charles Surface. Then, sir, my gratitude to the original is still increased.

Lady Teazle. Yet, I believe, Sir Oliver, here is one whom Charles is still more anxious to be reconciled to.

(*Pointing to* MARIA.)

Sir Oliver. Oh, I have heard of his attachment there; and, with the young lady's pardon, if I construe right—that blush—

Sir Peter. Well, child, speak your sentiments.

Maria. Sir, I have little to say, but that I shall rejoice to hear that he is happy; for me, whatever claim I had to his attention, I willingly resign to one who has a better title.

Charles Surface. How, Maria!

Sir Peter. Heyday! what's the mystery now? While he appeared an incorrigible rake, you would give your hand to no one else; and now that he is likely to reform I'll warrant you won't have him.

Maria. His own heart and Lady Sneerwell know the cause.

Charles Surface. Lady Sneerwell!

Joseph Surface. Brother, it is with great concern I am obliged to speak on this point, but my regard to justice compels me, and Lady Sneerwell's injuries can no longer be concealed. (*Opens the door.*)

Enter LADY SNEERWELL.

Sir Peter. So! another French milliner! Egad, he has one in every room in the house, I suppose!

Lady Sneerwell. Ungrateful Charles! Well may you be surprised, and feel for the indelicate situation your perfidy has forced me into.

Charles Surface. Pray, uncle, is this another plot of yours? For, as I have life, I don't understand it.

Joseph Surface. I believe, sir, there is but the evidence of one person more necessary to make it extremely clear.

Sir Peter. And that person, I imagine, is Mr. Snake. Row-

ley, you were perfectly right to bring him with us, and pray
let him appear.

Rowley. Walk in, Mr. Snake.

Enter SNAKE.

I thought his testimony might be wanted; however, it happens
unluckily, that he comes to confront Lady Sneerwell, not to
support her.

Lady Sneerwell. A villain! Treacherous to me at last! Speak,
fellow, have you too conspired against me?

Snake. I beg your ladyship ten thousand pardons: you
paid me extremely liberally for the lie in question; but I
unfortunately have been offered double to speak the truth.

Sir Peter. Plot and counterplot, egad!

Lady Sneerwell. The torments of shame and disappointment on you all!

Lady Teazle. Hold, Lady Sneerwell—before you go, let
me thank you for the trouble you and that gentleman have
taken in writing letters from me to Charles, and answering
them yourself; and let me also request you to make my re-
spects to the scandalous college, of which you are president,
and inform them that Lady Teazle, licentiate, begs leave to
return the diploma they granted her, as she leaves off prac-
tice and kills characters no longer.

Lady Sneerwell. You too, madam!—provoking—insolent!
May your husband live these fifty years!   *Exit.*

Sir Peter. Oons! what a fury!

Lady Teazle. A malicious creature, indeed!

Sir Peter. Hey! not for her last wish?

Lady Teazle. Oh, no!

Sir Oliver. Well, sir, and what have you to say now?

Joseph Surface. Sir, I am so confounded, to find that Lady
Sneerwell could be guilty of suborning Mr. Snake in this
manner, to impose on us all, that I know not what to say;
however, lest her revengeful spirit should prompt her to in-
jure my brother, I had certainly better follow her directly.
                                                            Exit.

Sir Peter. Moral to the last drop!

Sir Oliver. Ay, and marry her, Joseph, if you can. Oil and
vinegar—egad, you'll do very well together.

Rowley. I believe we have no more occasion for Mr.
Snake at present?

Snake. Before I go, I beg pardon once for all, for whatever uneasiness I have been the humble instrument of causing to the parties present.

Sir Peter. Well, well, you have made atonement by a good deed at last.

Snake. But I must request of the company, that it shall never be known.

Sir Peter. Hey! what the plague! are you ashamed of having done a thing right once in your life?

Snake. Ah, sir, consider—I live by the badness of my character; I have nothing but my infamy to depend on; and, if it were once known that I had been betrayed into an honest action, I should lose every friend I have in the world.

Sir Oliver. Well, well—we'll not traduce you by saying anything in your praise, never fear.   *Exit* SNAKE.

Sir Peter. There's a precious rogue!

Lady Teazle. See, Sir Oliver, there needs no persuasion now to reconcile your nephew and Maria.

Sir Oliver. Ay, ay, that's as it should be; and, egad, we'll have the wedding tomorrow morning.

Charles Surface. Thank you, dear uncle.

Sir Peter. What, you rogue! don't you ask the girl's consent first?

Charles Surface. Oh, I have done that a long time—a minute ago—and she has looked yes.

Maria. For shame, Charles!—I protest, Sir Peter, there has not been a word——

Sir Oliver. Well, then, the fewer the better: may your love for each other never know abatement.

Sir Peter. And may you live as happily together as Lady Teazle and I intend to do!

Charles Surface. Rowley, my old friend, I am sure you congratulate me; and I suspect that I owe you much.

Sir Oliver. You do, indeed, Charles.

Rowley. If my efforts to serve you had not succeeded, you would have been in my debt for the attempt—but deserve to be happy—and you overpay me.

Sir Peter. Ay, honest Rowley always said you would reform.

Charles Surface. Why as to reforming, Sir Peter, I'll make no promises, and that I take to be a proof that I intend to set about it. But here shall be my monitor—my gentle guide. —Ah! can I leave the virtuous path those eyes illumine?

Though thou, dear maid, shouldst wave thy beauty's sway,
Thou still must rule, because I will obey:
An humble fugitive from Folly view,
No sanctuary near but Love—and you: (*To the audience.*)
You can, indeed, each anxious fear remove,
For even Scandal dies, if you approve.

BY MR. COLMAN.

Spoken by LADY TEAZLE.

I, who was late so volatile and gay,
Like a trade-wind must now blow all one way,
Bend all my cares, my studies, and my vows,
To one dull rusty weathercock—my spouse!
So wills our virtuous bard—the motley Bayes[43]
Of crying epilogues and laughing plays!
Old bachelors, who marry smart young wives—
Learn from our play to regulate your lives:
Each bring his dear to town, all faults upon her—
London will prove the very source of honor.
Plunged fairly in, like a cold bath it serves,
When principles relax, to brace the nerves.
Such is my case; and yet I must deplore
That the gay dream of dissipation's o'er.
And say, ye fair! was ever lively wife,
Born with a genius for the highest life,
Like me untimely blasted in her bloom,
Like me condemned to such a dismal doom?
Save money—when I just knew how to waste it!
Leave London—just as I began to taste it!
Must I then watch the early-crowing cock,
The melancholy ticking of a clock;
In a lone rustic hall for ever pounded,[44]
With dogs, cats, rats, and squalling brats surrounded?
With humble curate can I now retire,
(While good Sir Peter boozes with the squire,)
And at backgammon mortify my soul,
That pants for loo, or flutters at a vole.[45]
Seven's the main![46] Dear sound that must expire,
Lost at hot cockels[47] round a Christmas fire;
The transient hour of fashion too soon spent,
Farewell the tranquil mind, farewell content![48]
Farewell the pluméd head, the cushioned tête,
That takes the cushion from its proper seat!
That spirit-stirring drum—card drums I mean,
Spadille—odd trick—pam—basto—king and queen!
And you, ye knockers that with brazen throat
The welcome visitors' approach denote;
Farewell all quality of high renown,

Pride, pomp, and circumstance of glorious town!
Farewell! your revels I partake no more,
And Lady Teazle's occupation's o'er!
All this I told our bard; he smiled, and said 'twas clear,
I ought to play deep tragedy next year.
Meanwhile he drew wise morals from his play,
And in these solemn periods stalked away:—
"Blessed were the fair like you; her faults who stopped.
And closed her follies when the curtain dropped!
No more in vice or error to engage.
Or play the fool at large on life's great stage."

NOTES TO

SHE STOOPS TO CONQUER

by Oliver Goldsmith

The leading theatrical figures of 18th century London had strong misgivings about the possible success of *She Stoops to Conquer*. However, through the influence of Samuel Johnson, it was prepared for production. Rehearsals were hectic and two of the leading comic actors of the time, Woodward and Smith, withdrew from the cast, saying they did not wish to be associated with a failure. Despite these difficulties the play opened at Covent Garden on March 15, 1773. A claque of Goldsmith's friends, led by Dr. Johnson, helped direct the enthusiasm of the audience and *She Stoops to Conquer* scored a deep and lasting success.

1. *Mr.* Woodward—A popular London actor. Woodward declined the part of Tony and hence does not appear in the original cast.

2. *Shuter*—"Ned" Shuter played Hardcastle in the original production of *She Stoops to Conquer*. He also appeared as Croaker in Goldsmith's *The Good-Natured Man*.

3. *Darby and Joan*—Traditionally, the happy old couple, as in eighteenth century ballads.

4. *Jorum*—A drinking bowl.

5. *"Water Parted"*—A song from Arne's opera *Antaxerxes*. *Ariadne* is an opera by Handel.

6. *Duchess of Drury Lane*—A prostitute.

7. *Us that sell ale*—Ordinary people.

8. *Ally Cawn*—Hyder Ali and Ali Khan were Indian Sultans. "Ally Croaker" was a popular Irish song.

9. *Florentine*—A meat pie. Shaking pudding is a jelly; taffety cream a rich creamy dessert.

10. *India Director*—An officer of the East India Company.

11. *St. James and Ranelagh are fashionable resorts of the nobility*—Tower Wharf is in a thoroughly disreputable section of London. The same disparity is found in Mrs. Hardcastle's allusions.

12. *Tête-à-tête*—Biographical sketches of people involved in society scandals published in *Town and Country* or similar magazines.

13. *Inoculation*—Smallpox inoculation was introduced in 1718.

14. *Quincy*—Dr. John Quincy was author of the *Complete English Dispensatory*.

15. *Mauvaise honte*—Self-consciousness.

16. *Bully Dawson*—A notorious ruffian.

17. *Cracker*—Fire cracker.

18. *Morrice*—A Morrice Dance: hence, "dance away."

19. *Marcasites*—Iron pyrites or fool's gold.

20. *Rose and table cut*—Relatively unfaceted gems, so cut because they are too small to be cut into the more highly faceted brilliants.

21. *Catharine wheel*—A revolving piece of fireworks; a pinwheel.

22. *Cherry in the "Beaux' Stratagem"*—The innkeeper's daughter in Farquhar's play.

23. *Lion, Angel, Lamb*—Imaginary names of inn-rooms.

24. *Tablets*—A memo pad.

25. *Seven, ames ace*—In hazard, winning and losing throws of dice. Ames ace, or both aces, is the lowest throw; American colloquialism, "snake eyes."

26. *"The Rake's Progress"*—One of Hogarth's famous series of engravings.

27. *Dullissimo Maccaroni*—A dull-witted dandy.

28. *Haspicholls*—Harpsichord.

29. *Baskets*—Basket-hilted rapiers; swords with shielded handles.

30. *But you know . . . her own disposal*—Early editions give this speech to Mrs. Hardcastle or omit it entirely. "Ay, but he's not of age . . ." was assigned to Mr. Hardcastle.

31. *Nancy Dawson*—A popular song.

32. *'Che Faro'*—An aria from Gluck's opera *Orfeo*.

33. *Heinel*—A fashionable German dancer.

34. *Spadille*—The ace of spades, in ombre or quadrille.

35. *Bayes*—The author in *The Rehearsal* by George Villers.

THE SCHOOL FOR SCANDAL

by Richard Brinsley Sheridan

The first production of this comedy was the result of many years of painstaking work. Using his well developed skills, Sheridan cleverly combined elements of two of his earlier plays, *The Slanderers* and *The Teazles* and composed *The School for Scandal*. The staging was also done with the greatest possible care. The first performance at Drury Lane on May 8, 1777 was acclaimed as a superb performance of a brilliant comedy.

1. *Quantum sufficit*—Plenty.

2. *Poz*—Positively.

3. *Sir Toby Bumper*—This character was omitted from the original cast of characters. In some later editions he is identified as Sir Harry Bumper.

4. *Tête-à-tête in the Town and Country Magazine*—Sketches of people involved in society scandals.

5. *City knight*—A knighted merchant.

6. *Diligence*—A public stagecoach.

7. *Laura*—The lady of Petrarch's sonnet cycle. Sacharissa is the name which Waller used to address Lady Dorothy Sidney.

8. *Tontine*—Annuities sold by act of the Irish parliament. The system was named for its originator, Lorenzo Tonti.

9. *Doubt*—Doubt not.

10. *Pantheon*—A fashionable concert hall.

11. *Fête champêtre*—A garden party.

12. *Tambour*—Embroidery frame.

13. *Pope Joan*—An unfashionable game of cards.

14. *Vis-à-vis*—A stylish carriage in which the occupants face each other.

15. *White cats*—Ponies.

16. *Macaronies*—Elegantly groomed ponies.

17. *Ring*—A drive in Hyde Park.

18. *French fruit*—Artificial fruits containing maxims printed on slips of paper; similar to the modern Chinese "fortune cookies."

19. *Law Merchant*—Mercantile law, under which endorsers assume responsibility for debts if the principals fail to pay.

20. *Cicisbeo*—A married woman's lover.

21. *Bluff*—Firm, staunch.

22. *a tear for pity*. . . . *"Henry IV,"* Part II, IV, iv, 31-32.

23. *Annuity Bill*—Designed to protect minors against unscrupulous sellers of annuities.

24. *Bags and bouquets*—Footman's livery. The bag wig, which used a small pouch to hold the hair, was fashionable at the time.

25. *Post-obit*—To take effect after death.

26. *Quean*—A harlot.

27. *Bough pots*—Window boxes.

28. *Race cups, corporation bowls*—Trophies and testimonial awards.

29. *Malplaquet*—Marlborough defeated the French forces, but suffered as many casualties as his opponents.

30. *Kneller*—Sir Godfrey Kneller, a fashionable portrait painter.

31. *Wool sack*—A symbol of the law. The Lord Chancellor's seat is the Woolsack—originally chosen as the emblem of Britain's wealth.

32. *Birthday clothes*—Elegant garments worn at the king's birthday celebration.

33. *Rupees, pagodas*—Coins of India.

34. *Congou tea*—A black Chinese tea.

35. *Avadavats*—Small Indian songbirds.

36. *Indian crackers*—Fire-crackers.

37. *Seconde*—A position in parrying.

38. *Montem*—A carnival, called the Montem, is held every third year on Whit-Tuesday, by the boys of Eton. The festivities take place on Salthill.

39. *Double letter*—An overweight letter requiring extra postage.

40. *Faculty*—The medical profession.

41. *Diffidence*—Doubt.

42. *A. B. at the coffee-house*—Appointments made under fictitious initials or concealed names.

43. *Bayes*—The author in *The Rehearsal* by George Villers.

44. *Pounded*—Confined.

45. *Loo*—A fashionable card game of the eighteenth century; vole: to win all the tricks in a deal.

46. *Seven's the main*—In the game of hazard, seven is one of the easiest "points" to throw.

47. *Hot cockles*—A juvenile game.

48. *This and the next ten lines parody "Othello,"* III, iii, 347-357.

"*Isn't there something that can make the literary classics more interesting?*"

Yes! The editors of Bantam Pathfinder Editions decided to publish the kind of aids to understanding and appreciation that you have been looking for. In special new editions are these four great classics of literature:

THE SCARLET LETTER	FP91 50¢
HUCKLEBERRY FINN	HP93 60¢
IDYLLS OF THE KING	HP92 60¢
BILLY BUDD, FORETOPMAN	FP90 50¢

Professional educators have designed each book to help you have a thorough understanding of the work and its place in literary history.

In addition to the complete and unabridged text, each edition provides these special features:

A detailed discussion of significant aspects
of theme, style, and structure.

Reviews, commentaries, and opinions.

Related background material.

A biographical sketch of the author.

UNFORGETTABLE READING

THE INCREDIBLE JOURNEY by SHEILA BURNFORD. The heart warming story of a Labrador retriever, a bull terrier, and a Siamese cat and their epic journey across the Canadian wilderness in the dead of winter to return to the family they love. 50c ☐

APRIL MORNING by HOWARD FAST. The exciting story of a young boy living in revolutionary America who suddenly becomes a man during the battle of Lexington. 50c ☐